S0-BNW-441

ASIAN HISTORICAL DICTIONARIES
Edited by Jon Woronoff

1. *Vietnam*, by William J. Duiker. 1989
2. *Bangladesh*, by Craig Baxter and Syedur Rahman. 1989

Historical Dictionary
of
BANGLADESH

by
CRAIG BAXTER
and
SYEDUR RAHMAN

Asian Historical Dictionaries, No. 2

The Scarecrow Press, Inc.
Metuchen, N.J., & London
1989

DS
394.5
B39
1989

British Library Cataloguing-in-Publication data available

ROBERT MANNING
STROZIER LIBRARY

SEP 8 1989

Tallahassee, Florida

Library of Congress Cataloging-in-Publication Data

Baxter, Craig.
   Historical dictionary of Bangladesh.

   (Asian historical dictionaries ; no. 2)
   Bibliography: p.
   1. Bangladesh--History--Dictionaries. I. Rahman,
Syedur. II. Title. III. Series.
DS394.5.B39 1989   954.9'2'00321   88-35946
ISBN 0-8108-2177-X

Copyright © 1989 by Craig Baxter and Syedur Rahman
Manufactured in the United States of America

CONTENTS

EDITOR'S FOREWORD

Bangladesh is certainly not one of the best-known Asian countries. And what is "known" about it is not always very favorable. It is usually presented in stories that stress its overpopulation and under-development. But there is much more to it than that. Bengal has a long and often-times proud tradition. It has produced writers and artists of genius. It is an important outpost of Islam. And, with a population of over a hundred million, it is one of the larger countries in the world. It therefore deserves to be known better by more people.

That is the purpose of this volume. But it was not easy to achieve given the great length and considerable complexity of the history of a place now called Bangladesh, but previously just East Pakistan, and before that part of British India, and so on into the past. It has been inhabited by different peoples, of different re-ligions and ruled over by different leaders who imposed different regimes. Yet, despite the difficulty of writing a "historical" dic-tionary, the effort succeeded. With its many entries, an enlightening introduction and an ample bibliography, we trust that this book will serve as an accessible point of entry for those new to the country and still a source of useful information for the more experienced.

This Asian Historical Dictionary was produced by two leading authorities. One is Craig Baxter, a retired foreign service officer and now Professor of Politics and History at Juniata College, whose long familiarity with the country and the region was refreshed by a recent trip. He is the author of one of the few topical works, Bangladesh, A New Nation in an Old Setting. The other is Syedur Rahman, born and educated in Bangladesh, who has taught at the University of Dhaka and is now Assistant Professor of Public Ad-ministration at the Pennsylvania State University. He has written, inter alia, on regional cooperation in South Asia.

Jon Woronoff
Series Editor

CHRONOLOGY OF IMPORTANT EVENTS

1500 B.C.	Approximate date of arrival of Indo-Aryans in the Indus valley.
1000 B.C.	Approximate date of arrival of Bang tribe in the lower Ganges valley.
273-232 B.C.	Reign of Maurya emperor Ashoka
320-510 A.D.	Gupta dynasty
606-647	Reign of Harsha.
750	Founding of Pala dynasty.
1150	Fall of Pala dynasty. Beginning of Sena dynasty.
1202	Fall of Sena capital, Nadia, to Khalji general representing Ghurid dynasty.
1336	Rebellion against Tughluq dynasty of Delhi sultanate led by Fakhruddin Mubarak Shah.
1346	After decade of turmoil, Shamsuddin Iliyas Shah founded Iliyas Shahi dynasty.
1490	Overthrow of Iliyas Shahi dynasty. Founding of Sayyid dynasty.
1517	Arrival of Portuguese in Chittagong.
1538	Conquest of Bengal by troops of the Mughal emperor Humayun.
1539	Rebels under Sher Shah Suri, an Afghan, take Bengal and rule to 1564.
1564	Rival Afghan dynasty won control of Bengal.
1576	Conquest of Bengal by Mughal emperor Akbar.

1608	Dhaka became capital of Mughal's Bengal province.
1650	Arrival of British in Bengal.
1686	British found Calcutta.
1704	Murshidabad became capital.
1756	Mughal governor Sirajuddaulah attacked Calcutta. Incident of the "Black Hole."
1757	British under Clive defeated Sirajuddaulah at Battle of Plassey.
1765	Robert Clive governor of Bengal (to 1767).
1772	Warren Hastings as governor. Became governor general in 1773.
1793	Permanent Settlement decreed by Cornwallis.
1857	Sepoy Mutiny.
1858	Transfer of power from British East India Company to the Crown. Queen Victoria's proclamation that all subjects are equal under the law.
1861	India Councils Act permitted inclusion of Indians in legislative councils of the lieutenant governors and the governor general.
1883	Local Councils Act permitted limited election to local government boards.
1885	Indian National Congress founded at Bombay.
1894	India Councils Act expanded rights given in 1861 act.
1905	Partition of Bengal.
1906	Muslim delegation met Lord Minto at Simla. Muslim League founded in Dhaka.
1909	Government of India Act (Morley-Minto Act) granted Muslim demand of separate electorates and further expanded powers of legislative councils.
1911	Annulment of partition of Bengal. Capital of India transferred from Calcutta to New Delhi.
1919	Government of India Act (Montagu-Chelmsford Act) created system of dyarchy at provincial level.

1935   Government of India Act provided for provincial autonomy and responsible government. Proposed changes at federal level were not fully implemented as Indian princes would not accept subordination to dyarchical system at that level.

1937   Provincial elections held. Fazlul Haq became first prime minister of Bengal.

1940   March 23. Muslim League passed "Pakistan Resolution" at Lahore proposing that partition of India may be necessary.

1941   Fazlul Haq left Muslim League but his prime ministership continued.

1943   Muslim League ministry headed by Nazimuddin formed.

1945   New elections held. Muslim League formed ministry headed by Suhrawardy.

1947   August 15. Partition of India and independence of dominions of India and Pakistan. Muslim League formed ministry in East Bengal headed by Nazimuddin.

1951   Nazimuddin became governor general of Pakistan. Nurul Amin headed East Bengal ministry.

1952   February 21. Martyrs' day in memory of students killed in pro-Bengali language demonstrations in Dhaka.

1954   Muslim League trounced by United Front of Awami League (Suhrawardy) and Krishak Sramik Party (KSP) (Fazlul Haq). Fazlul Haq became chief minister briefly but central government imposed governor's rule (to 1956).

1955   East Bengal renamed East Pakistan.

1956   First Pakistani constitution effective on March 23.

1956-1958   United Front having broken apart, Awami League and KSP alternated leadership of government during increasingly tumultuous period.

1958   President Mirza declared martial law on October 7. General Muhammad Ayub Khan dismissed Mirza on October 28 and assumed presidency.

1962   Ayub proclaimed second constitution including for-
               malization of system of basic democracies (operative
               since 1959). Martial law ended.

1965   War between Pakistan and India in September.

1966   Sheikh Mujibur Rahman announced Awami League
               Six-Point Program.

1969   March 25. Ayub resigned and turned presidency
               over to General Yahya Khan. Martial law reimposed.

1970   December. Elections held in Pakistan. Awami
               League won 160 of 162 national assembly seats from
               East Pakistan, but none of 138 from West Pakistan.

1971   Constitutional talks among Yahya, Mujib and Bhutto
               failed. On March 25, Pakistan army moved against
               Bengalis. Civil war broke out. Indians took sur-
               render of Dhaka to allied forces on December 16.
               Indian forces entered conflict in late November.

1972   Mujib, who had been in captivity in West Pakistan,
               returned to Dhaka January 10. On December 16,
               Bangladesh constitution promulgated.

1973   Elections to Bangladesh parliament gave Awami
               League 292 of 300 seats.

1975   Mujib assassinated on August 15. Khondakar Mush-
               taque Ahmad became president. Insurrection Novem-
               ber 3-5 led by Khalid Musharaf failed. Ziaur Rahman
               emerged as key figure. A.S.M. Sayem named presi-
               dent.

1977   Zia replaced Sayem as president on April 21. Won
               referendum to hold office on May 30.

1978   Zia elected president and Abdus Sattar appointed
               vice president on June 3.

1979   Parliamentary election gave Zia's party 207 of 300 seats.

1981   Zia assassinated on May 30. Sattar became acting
               president. Sattar elected president on November 15.

1982   Sattar overthrown in military coup led by H. M.
               Ershad on March 24.

1986   Parliamentary election gave Ershad's party a slight
               majority. Awami League and its allies won about 1/3
               of the seats.

INTRODUCTION

Bangladesh (literally, the land of the Bengalis) is the most recent addition (in 1971) to the independent nations of South Asia. The term "South Asia" is usually defined now as including the seven states which are members of the South Asian Association for Regional Co-operation (SAARC): Bangladesh, Bhutan, India, the Maldives, Nepal, Pakistan and Sri Lanka. In academic usage the term may also include Afghanistan. These states are ones that were under British control or influence throughout much of the 19th and early 20th centuries. Those controlled directly by the British attained independence in 1947 (India and Pakistan), 1948 (Sri Lanka, then Ceylon) and 1971 (Bangladesh, but from Pakistan not Britain). They, therefore, share a heritage in such areas as administration, legal systems and many political structures. They also share a traditional background although Hinduism, which still dominates in India (and Nepal), has long since been superseded by Islam in Pakistan and Bangladesh and Buddhism in Sri Lanka.

The recent separation of Bangladesh from Pakistan and the partition of India in 1947 make it evident that there will be much overlap among the works in this series on the three countries. A further complication is that the term "Bangladesh" itself is a misnomer. While Bangladesh contains a majority of the speakers of the Bengali language, there are many more who live in and give their name to the Indian state of West Bengal and others in fair numbers in the state of Assam, also in India.

Geography

Bangladesh is a compact country, comprising mainly the deltaic area formed by the mouths of the combined Ganges (Ganga) and Brahmaputra rivers that rise respectively in India and Tibet. To these rivers is added another major stream, the Meghna, which rises in the northeastern part of Bangladesh itself. The region is thus an alluvial plain with but few exceptions. These include the hills in the northeastern portion (Sylhet Region) where rainfall occurs at one of the highest rates in the world, and the eastern area (Chittagong Hill Tracts Region) with lower but still substantial rainfall. (It should be noted that the political units once known as "districts" have now been reclassified as "regions," and those formerly known as "subdivisions" as "districts.")

1

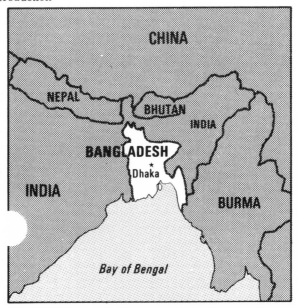

The combination of the usually heavy monsoon rainfall and the flow from the rivers resulting from upstream snow melt provides Bangladesh with a quantity of water that can be both a blessing and a curse. On the positive side, the annual flooding provides water for the growing of such water-demanding crops as rice and jute and also replenishes the fertile soil with deposits of silt brought from the Himalaya and the Tibetan plateau. The streams also provide an intricate network of routes for domestic travel and commerce, but, of course, at the same time they act as formidable barriers to the development of road and rail transport. The continual migration of the rivers and streams makes bridging a difficult task, while the major rivers have also inhibited the distribution of electricity and of the natural gas which is abundant in the country. Another serious "curse" is the frequent extensive flooding that, rather than contributing to agriculture, washes away crops, kills animals and often people, and destroys villages.

Although there are dangers from an excess of water, Bangladesh is clearly heavily dependent on the flow of the rivers. The withdrawals of water from the Ganges by the upper riparian, India, has diminished the flow into Bangladesh. This has been demonstrated most clearly in the building of a barrage at Farakka, just upstream from the border, by India with the purpose of diverting Ganges water through the Bhagirati and Hooghly rivers to assist the city of Calcutta. An important and unresolved political dispute between India and Bangladesh has resulted, although there has been a temporary agreement to divide the water roughly evenly during the low flow period in April, May and June. India has proposed a link canal

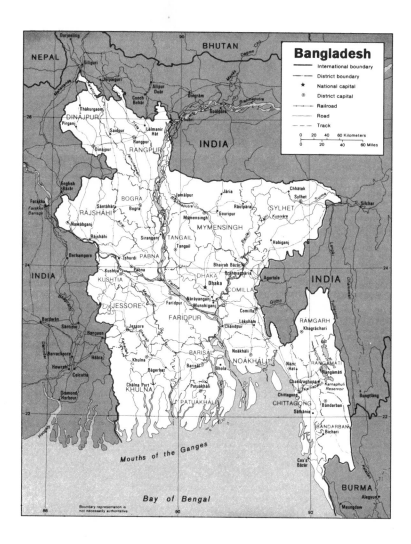

to move water from the Brahmaputra (which usually has an excess flow to the needs downstream) to a point upstream from Farakka to augment the low season flow. Bangladesh has objected, as the canal would have both its intake and outflow under Indian control but would flow for most of its length in Bangladesh. Bangladesh has proposed a tripartite arrangement which would include Nepal and result in additional storage dams on Nepali territory.

The rivers flow slowly through Bangladesh. Dhaka, for example, is only 24 feet above sea level. Therefore, there is but limited potential for hydroelectric generation. The only exception, so far, is the harnessing of the Karnaphuli River upstream from Chittagong for power.

Bangladesh is also subject to another climatic phenomenon that can only be destructive: the cyclones which arise in the Bay of Bengal and cause damage in eastern India as well as Bangladesh. The great cyclone of 1970 may have killed as many as half a million people along the coastal areas and left countless more injured and homeless. Construction of homes from more permanent materials and the development, perhaps through SAARC, of extensive early warning programs could help to ameliorate such widespread damage. The building of polders, with Dutch assistance, has also been effective in some areas.

Bangladesh's borders are neither traditional nor natural. The land boundary is almost entirely with India, the exception being in the very southeastern end of the country where it borders on the Arakan area of Burma. As will be noted below, the border with India was set in 1947 as part of the process of partitioning British India. The result has been the leaving of enclaves on one side or the other and another political problem between the two countries.

The southern boundary is the Bay of Bengal but the exact location of that boundary is still a matter of dispute between India and Bangladesh. The appearance of new islands in the bay has complicated the negotiations as has the law of the sea agreement. Bangladesh as a state at the end of an indenture in the sea is not accorded an economic zone of 200 miles as this zone must be plotted on a line which respects also the rights of Burma and India. The definition of the ownership of new islands would affect the base points from which the economic zone is determined.

The People

The 102 million people of Bangladesh are crowded into an area of 55,126 square miles (about the size of Wisconsin). This gives the country a population density of more than 1,800 per square mile, higher than any state except for such city-states as Singapore and Hong Kong. Although there has been some progress in the family planning program, the growth rate was 2.6 per cent (1980-1985) and a population of 141 million is forecasted for the end of the century. Such overcrowding has, of course, important economic and social implications which will be noted in the next section.

The rate of urbanization has been lower in Bangladesh than in most third-world countries. More than 80 percent of the population is classified as rural. Dhaka, with 3.5 million (1981), is the largest city. Only one other city has a population higher than one million, Chittagong with 1.4 million (1981).

The vast majority of the people are Bengalis, a branch of the Indo-Aryans who migrated to the eastern areas of the subcontinent after the earlier movement of the group from Central Asia to the region of the Indus River in the second millenium before Christ. Prior to their arrival, the region seems to have been populated by Dravidian groups, whose physical characteristics of shorter stature and darker skin are seen in the mixed population of Bangladesh. Evidence of some Mongoloid background can also be seen in eastern Bangladesh, especially in the regions of Sylhet and Chittagong.

About 85 percent of the Bangladeshis are Muslim, almost all of the Sunni branch. These include a small proportion who are descendants of Muslims who migrated from north India to serve as officers of the Delhi sultanate or the Mughal empire and remained in Bengal. The bulk, however, were converted, usually through Sufi preachers, from among the population already resident in the area. For reasons which are not clear, the rate of conversion was higher in the eastern parts of Bengal than the western and this was recognized when the united province of Bengal was partitioned in 1947.

Most of the remaining 15 percent of the population is Hindu. Among them, the majority belong to the Scheduled Castes (a legal term for those formerly known as Untouchables). The bulk of the upper-caste Hindus fled to India by the early 1950s or later, at the time of the civil war in 1971. Generally, the western districts of Bangladesh have a higher percentage of Hindus than the eastern.

The other Bangladeshis are Christian (a few hundred thousand) or Buddhist. Many of each group are tribals. Christian tribals (e.g., Garos, Khasis) are often southern extensions of groups whose main territory is in the Indian state of Meghalaya, north of Bangladesh. Buddhist tribals are most often found in the Chittagong Hill Tracts (e.g., Chakmas, Tripuras). Many of the latter group have been in rebellion against the Bangladesh government, asserting that "flat landers" have moved into the reserved hill areas. Some tribals, however, are Hindus or animists.

A special group among the Muslims are known as Biharis, who numbered about 600,000 in 1971. These are Urdu-speaking Muslims who fled India in 1947 eastward to what was then East Bengal, rather than westward as most Muslim refugees did. Unable and perhaps un-willing to integrate with their Bengali-speaking co-religionists, the group strongly supported the retention of a united Pakistan. They were, therefore, looked upon as a kind of fifth column by the Bangla-deshi nationalists. Since 1971, some (usually younger persons) have been able to integrate, some have been sent to Pakistan or have made their own way there, but others remain in camps awaiting transporta-tion to Pakistan. The story of the Biharis has received great at-tention in the media.

Bangladesh is the only South Asia state which is unilingual; almost all Bangladeshis have Bengali as their mother tongue. The language is derived from Sanskrit, the most eastern of the Indo-European languages. It is written in a script that is a modification of the Sanskrit writing system and is closely akin to the script of Hindi. Early modern contributions to the rich Bengali literature have been mainly the product of Hindu writers, including the No-belist Rabindranath Tagore. More recently, Muslims have also added to the literary tradition with the works of such writers as Kazi Nazrul Islam. During the period of Sheikh Mujibur Rahman, great emphasis was placed on Bengalization of all activity, but since then English has revived as a key language of international communica-tions and commerce, although often neglected in the educational sys-tem.

The Economy

In terms of per capita gross national product (GNP), Bangla-desh is among the poorest nations in the world. According to data collected by the World Bank for 1985, GNP/per capita was $150. Equity, as measured by income distribution, was badly skewed in 1981-1982, the latest year for which figures are available: the high-est 20 percent of the population received about 45 percent of the in-come, while the lowest 20 percent received but 6.6 percent. It has been said with good reason that 60-75 percent of the population of Bangladesh lives below the poverty line. The rural population prob-ably has a higher rate of poverty than the urban. Agriculture, which employed 75 percent of the working labor force, produced only 50 percent of the GNP. The share of industry in the GNP was only 14 percent.

The economy of Bangladesh, therefore, is based almost entire-ly on agricultural products. For domestic consumption the key is rice; for international trade it is jute, a fiber used in such products as burlap and carpeting (as backing) but one which has a diminishing market partly as the result of the development of synthetic fibers. These products are grown on very small plots of land. There is a land ceiling, but this means little to most Bangladeshis, as the aver-age land holding among those with land was 3.5 acres in 1977. If the rural landless family units are factored into the calculation, the average drops to 2.3 acres. In addition, owing to inheritance patterns, a holding may be divided into as many as 20 or more fragments. Offsetting this to a limited degree is the ability in some areas to till the land two or three times a year; 38 percent of the land is double-cropped and 7 percent triple-cropped.

Campaigns to intensify production, especially of rice, have had some effect. Production of this cereal did not reach pre-independence levels of just more than 10 million tons until the 1973-74 crop year, but by 1982-83 the production surpassed 15 million tons. Nonetheless, the production of this staple is less than one pound per person per day, and, even assuming equitable distribution, this means a nutritional deficiency. Bangladesh must receive additional supplies (often wheat rather than the preferred rice) either through purchase or through international assistance programs.

Industrial growth has been inhibited by a lack of raw materials, a shortage of investment capital, an untrained labor force, an early policy of nationalization, and frequent periods of political instability. More recently, the government has privatized many industrial units and has enacted a more liberal investment policy for both domestic and foreign investors but, at this writing, this has had little effect on investment patterns. An offsetting factor has been the migration of Bangladeshi workers to the Middle East. While this has accentuated shortages of trained labor in several fields, it has resulted in remittances by overseas workers of about one half billion dollars a year. However, with the decline in world oil prices, this amount has also declined although not as sharply as once anticipated.

The infrastructure is weak. The division of the country by the rivers has made the linking of the electrical grids impossible so far. This is also true of gas transmission lines from the east to the west. Projects are now in hand to overcome both these deficiencies. The use of the abundant domestic natural gas would help offset the growing cost of imported petroleum. As mentioned earlier, highway and railway networks are also hindered by the rivers and the use of small boats for industrial traffic is not entirely satisfactory.

The future of the Bangladesh economy, particularly in view of the steadily growing population, is not bright. Bangladesh will need the assistance of international aid donors for many years to come.

Early History

One of the leading British historians of India said in the early part of this century: "No definite affirmation of any kind can be made about specific events in ... Bengal before 300 B.C." Since he wrote there have been no discoveries which would change that statement. Unlike the Indus valley in the western part of the subcontinent where a developed civilization existed prior to the arrival of the Indo-Aryans, no archaeological remains have been found to suggest the existence of a similar civilization in the lower Ganges valley. There are references to Vanga in early Sanskrit literature (the "b" and "v" are interchanged) and it is thought that an Indo-Aryan tribe, the Bang (or Vang), moved to the Bengal area in the beginning of the first millenium before Christ. The tribe, it is believed, gave its name to the area.

Bengal formed the eastern extremity of the empire built by Chandragupta Maurya in the fourth century B.C. and expanded by his grandson, Ashoka, in the third century B.C. A seaport (near Tamluk in West Bengal) was developed and, in addition to trade, it may have served as the point from which Buddhism was spread to Ceylon and Southeast Asia.

When the Mauryan empire collapsed shortly after the death of Ashoka, Bengal was left very much on its own. Local rulers presumably held sway, although Bengal paid tribute to the Gupta empire in the 4th and 5th centuries A.D. During this period, eastern Bengal was dominated by the kingdom of Samatata (located near the present city of Chandpur). In the 7th century, Samatata was drawn briefly into the shortlived Gupta revival empire of Harsha. In any event, during the long period from the Mauryas to Harsha, Bengal was very much a backwater as far as the rulers who dominated the heartland of India were concerned.

In 750 Bengal produced a dynasty which would spread its control over areas outside Bengal itself. This was the Pala dynasty which ruled, at times with difficulty, until 1150. As its power moved westward it faced challenges from other kingdoms in India which had the same goal of reconstructing the empire of Harsha. Also as it expanded, its base moved westward from Bengal and its capital became what is the present city of Monghyr in Bihar. The Pala capital within Bengal was Vikrampur in the neighborhood of Dhaka. The Palas were ardent Buddhists, descendants perhaps of those who had been converted from lower castes to Buddhism during the time of Ashoka.

As Pala power began to decline in the 11th and 12th centuries, it appeared that another group would inherit at least the Bengali portion of the empire. This came in 1150 when the last Pala (and Buddhist) ruler was overthrown by a tributary principality ruled by the Senas, a Hindu dynasty. In their brief career, the Senas worked to revive Brahmanism as the religion of Bengal, a task that alienated many of the common people who had welcomed casteless Buddhism and who would soon welcome equally casteless Islam in their aversion to the Brahmanical Hinduism of the Senas. In 1202 the last major Sena ruler was expelled from his capital at Nadia (now in West Bengal) by Muslims. Collateral branches of the Senas continued to rule for a short time in eastern Bengal, but the period of Islamic rule had begun in eastern India and would last until 1757.

Islamic Rule

The Muslims had entered India in the 8th century in Sind, but the major invasion which would change the political complexion of most of the subcontinent came at the beginning of the 11th century. Then Mahmud of Ghazni, a Turk, began a series of incursions from what is now Afghanistan. The Slave (Mamluk) dynasty was the first to rule from Delhi (1206-1290).

Ikhtiyaruddin Muhammad Bakhtiyar Khalji, representing the Ghurids (who had succeeded the Ghaznavids), attacked Bengal between 1198 and 1201, conquering Nadia in 1202. During the next 50 years, eastern Bengal would also come under control of the Slave dynasty of the Delhi sultanate and the surviving Sena rulers would be eliminated. He established the capital of the region at Gaur, now a ruined site near Malda in West Bengal. Until Dhaka was established as the capital in 1608, Gaur and its neighbors Pandua and Tanda would serve almost continuously as the seat of government of Bengal.

Under the Khalji dynasty (1290-1320) in Delhi, Bengal remained a province of the sultanate. The sultanate reached its greatest power under the Tughluq dynasty (1320-1413), but the period also saw the beginnings of the disintegration of the sultanate. During the early years of the reign of Muhammad bin Tughluq (1325-1351), the territory ruled by the sultanate reached its greatest extent, but by the time his reign ended much had been lost. Independent kingdoms were established in a number of areas including Gujarat, the Deccan, Malwa and Bengal.

The Bengal rebellion was begun in 1336 by Fakhruddin Mubarak Shah who ruled the area somewhat tentatively for about ten years. In the confused condition of Bengal, Shamsuddin Iliyas Shah came out the winner and established the Iliyas Shahi dynasty as independent rulers of Bengal. This dynasty was overthrown in 1490 by Alauddin Husain Shah. The Sayyid dynasty founded by him ruled until 1538.

A new force had arrived in Delhi which sought to reassemble the territories of the Delhi sultanate and expand them. The decaying Lodhi dynasty in Delhi was defeated on April 21, 1526, at Panipat, north of Delhi, by Babar, the leader of the group that would found the Mughal empire. Troops of his son, Humayan (reigned 1530-1540 and 1555-1556), conquered Bengal in 1538. However, Humayun faced a revolt from the Afghan Sher Shah Suri and his troops took Bengal in 1539. Although Humayun regained the throne shortly before his death, the region of Bengal remained under the rule of the successors of Sher Shah until 1564. Bengal continued to remain separate from Delhi under a new Afghan dynasty founded by Sulaiman Karnani.

The Mughal emperor Akbar (1556-1605) brought Bengal under imperial control in 1576 when his troops defeated Daud Khan, the second and last sultan of Bengal in the Afghan dynasty. From then until 1971, when a portion of Bengal became independent, Bengal would be under the control of non-Bengal-based rulers.

Bengal became a province (suba) of the Mughal empire and was ruled by a governor (naib nazim) appointed from Delhi. The power exercised by the governor was dependent on the strength of the Mughal court. After the death of the emperor Aurangzeb in 1707, the empire steadily declined in power; conversely, the relative independence of the governors in Dhaka (where the capital had moved in 1608) tended to increase. Furthermore, the governorship became hereditary. The capital was moved from Dhaka to Murshidabad (now in West Bengal) in 1704.

In the 16th century, Europeans began to arrive in Bengal. The Portuguese made their first settlement in Chittagong in 1517 and added a station at Hooghly, on the river of the same name, in 1579. The Dutch arrived in 1602 followed by the British in 1650. The French and the Danes would follow. The British founded Calcutta in 1686.

So long as the governors were backed by some measure of Mughal strength they were able to keep the Europeans in check and to regulate their activities reasonably well. In the early 18th century the system began to break down. A rebellion by Alivardi Khan, the deputy for Bihar to the governor, displaced the incumbent and Alivardi became governor until his death in 1756. His grandson and successor, Sirajuddaulah, would see his brief rule bring the British into effective power.

The British Period

The British had become the dominant European power in India, in the south through their defeat of the French and in Bengal with the decline of the Portuguese and the evident relative weakness of the French, Dutch and Danes. The British expanded their station at Calcutta and built trading networks with the local merchants. Sirajuddaulah then attacked Calcutta on June 20, 1756, and took Fort William. According to British reports, the captured British were placed in a room ("The Black Hole") in the fort and 123 of the 146 prisoners died of suffocation. The British determined to revenge the defeat and the deaths.

They were able to find persons in Sirajuddaulah's court, including a close relative, Mir Jafar, who would work with them. On June 23, 1757, at Plassey (Pilasi), a British force under the command of Robert Clive, defeated Sirajuddaulah, with the help of the treachery of Mir Jafar. Sirajuddaulah was executed on July 2, 1757; four days earlier the British recognized Mir Jafar as governor. In 1760

Mir Jafar was replaced by his son-in-law, Mir Qasim, but the latter was displaced in 1763 and Mir Jafar returned to office until his death in 1765.

In that same year, the British were granted the diwani (the right to collect and expend revenue) for Bengal, Bihar and Orissa by the Mughal emperor. The Bengal government was not well organized until Warren Hastings was appointed governor in 1772. The following year, Hastings became the first governor general of India, retaining the office of governor of Bengal and subordinating the other two major settlements, Bombay and Madras, to Calcutta. Calcutta would remain the capital of British India until 1911.

The dominance of Calcutta, however, tended to make the eastern portion of the province (the area which is now Bangladesh) a backwater. The permanent settlement initiated by Lord Cornwallis (governor general, 1786-1793 and again briefly in 1805) also contributed to the slower development of eastern Bengal. Bengal, under the Mughals and under the British, had used a system of tax collectors (zamindars) who collected land tax from the ryots (tillers) and remitted an amount to the government after keeping a share for their services. Under the new system introduced by Cornwallis in 1793, the zamindar was recognized as owner of the land from which he had collected taxes. The ryots then, for all practical purposes, became his tenants. The system would not be fully abolished in East Bengal until after independence. Most, but by no means all, of the zamindars in eastern Bengal were Hindus and most of the ryots Muslims. Gradually the zamindars became absentee landlords and most migrated to Calcutta to participate in the development of that city to the detriment of the rural areas of eastern Bengal.

Calcutta did indeed flourish. It became a center not only of government and commerce but also of the arts and literature and of reformist movements leading eventually to the demand for Indian independence. Dhaka, which had ceased to be the capital in 1704, languished and saw much of its industry, especially the manufacture of Dhaka muslin, decline. Calcutta became the seat of a university in 1857; Dhaka not until 1921. As we shall see, there was a brief revival when Dhaka became a capital again after the first partition of Bengal in 1905.

The British Indian army (actually that of the British East India Company) was comprised of three separate armies: Bengal, Bombay and Madras. The troops (sepoys) were Indian; the officers British. There were also units of the British army stationed in India, but these were separate from the British Indian army. The British Indian army had faced several outbreaks of mutiny in the early 19th century, but these were relatively small affairs and were put down quickly.

In 1857, however, the British faced a large-scale mutiny by

the Bengal army (Madras and Bombay did not join the mutineers).
It broke out in Meerut on May 10, 1857, although there had been unrest elsewhere before. Delhi fell to the sepoys and eventually was
recaptured. By early 1858, the mutiny was over but there would
result two decisions that would affect Bengal.

The British East India Company was formally wound up in 1858.
It had been severely circumscribed by a series of acts passed by
the British parliament beginning with the act that created the office
of governor general in 1773. In 1858, control of British India passed
from the company to the crown. Queen Victoria (she would be
designated Empress of India in 1877), in her proclamation, stated
that all of her subjects would be treated equally before the law. Although this declaration was never fully implemented, it served as
one step along the path of opening the system of governance to Indian participation. The governor general would now also hold the
title of viceroy.

A second outcome was the determination that India was populated by martial and nonmartial races. The Bengalis were in the latter category, as the British believed that the Bengalis were a major
element among the mutineers. This meant that recruitment for the
military was barred for Bengalis (except for some specialized personnel) and that the recruiting grounds moved to the northwest, to the
Sikhs and the Punjabi Muslims primarily. One of the grievances of
the East Pakistanis against the central government of Pakistan after
independence in 1947 would be the small share of Bengalis in the military as Pakistan continued the policy of the British with but small
change.

Bengal itself would be in the forefront of administrative changes
made by the British. It and some other provinces saw Indians appointed to the legislative councils of the lieutenant governors under
the provisions of the India Councils Act of 1861 and more under the
next edition of the act in 1894. The viceroyalty of Lord Ripon (1880-
1884), a liberal associate of Gladstone, saw several changes (implemented first in Bengal) including the establishment of local boards
at the subdivision level and district boards above them. Membership
was elective, subject to rather strict franchise requirements. The
bodies were permitted to raise and expend funds for such purposes
as education and public works. Ripon also repealed the act which
limited free expression in local language newspapers and gave those
newspapers equal status with those published in English. He attempted, but failed, to reform the judicial system so that Indian
judges would have the same right to try Europeans as British judges
did.

The Indian National Congress was founded in Bombay on December 28, 1885. The first president was a Bengali Hindu from Calcutta. For several reasons, Muslims did not associate with the Congress in large numbers. Part of this abstention came from the appeal

of a leading Muslim educationist, Sir Syed Ahmad Khan, who laid the seeds for the "Two Nation Theory" that would eventually be a source for the partition of India in 1947. Sir Syed and others who further developed the theory maintained that there was sufficient difference between the Hindus of India and the Muslims of India that they should be considered separate nations even though they inhabited the same territory. Sir Syed also feared that the departure of the British would result in a Hindu raj in which the Muslims would play a minor, if any, role and in which values held important by Muslims could be violated by a form of dictatorship of the majority. This theme, too, would be replayed as Indian independence approached.

The introduction of the elective principle by Ripon through his act on local government also concerned the Muslims. Even in areas where Muslims might be in a majority in the population, they could be outvoted as a result of the stringent franchise rules. These generally involved either property ownership or educational attainments. Perhaps in no place more than eastern Bengal would the Muslims find meeting franchise qualifications so difficult.

Muslims throughout India recognized this problem. It was brought to a head when it became apparent that the viceroy, Lord Minto (viceroy, 1905-1910), and the secretary of state for India in the British cabinet, Lord Morley, were determined that further constitutional advance for India should be enacted. The Muslims would take two steps, a meeting with Minto at Simla and the formation of the Muslim League.

Before these two events occurred, however, another event of great importance for eastern Bengal took place. The governor general/viceroy had been relieved of the direct administration of Bengal in 1854, when the province was placed under separate administration (the title for the head of the provincial government throughout India was then lieutenant governor, later to be changed to governor by the Government of India Act of 1909). Lord Curzon (viceroy, 1899-1905) determined that the large province of Bengal, which included Bihar and Orissa, was too unwieldy to be managed effectively. He partitioned the province so that Bengal itself was divided. The eastern portion of the province (roughly Bangladesh today) was joined with Assam into the province of Eastern Bengal and Assam; the remaining area became the province of Western Bengal, Bihar and Orissa; each had a lieutenant governor.

Bengali Hindus objected to the change. In the first place, it created a Muslim majority province in the east (only one other, the Punjab, existed at that time). With a view toward future elected governments at the provincial level, Hindus saw the danger of a Muslim raj much as Muslims saw the reverse on an all-India level. Second, those who spoke Bengali became a minority in the western province, being outnumbered by the total of the Hindi speakers of Bihar and the Oriya speakers of Orissa. Hindus reacted with measures that included violence and terrorism as well as less violent means such as a boycott of British goods. Noted Hindu Bengalis including the poet Tagore and the future religious leader but then revolutionary Aurobindo Ghose lent their voices and pens to the protest. The Muslims supported the partition and Dhaka temporarily revived from its backwater status to become a provincial capital.

The British eventually heeded the Hindu opposition and, to the great disappointment of the Muslims, revoked the partition of Bengal in 1911. The announcement was made during the imperial visit to India of King George V and Queen Mary. However, the annulment of the partition was coupled with an imperial decree transferring the capital of India from Calcutta to New Delhi. Under the new arrangement of provinces, Assam reverted to a separate status, eastern and western Bengal became the province of Bengal, and the remainder became the province of Bihar and Orissa (these two were separated under the Government of India Act of 1919).

During the partition period, as noted earlier, the Muslims were active politically. A delegation led by the Aga Khan met Lord Minto at Simla in 1906 and proposed a system of separate electorates under which seats would be apportioned in legislative bodies between Muslims and "others" in proportion to the two groups' shares in the population. In the election, Muslims and "others" would vote separately and only for representatives of their own community. (As the system developed later, other religious groups such as Sikhs and Indian Christians would also gain separate representation and electorates). The Muslim demand, a natural culmination of the "Two Nation Theory," was incorporated into the Government of India Act of 1909 (the "Morley-Minto Act"). Separate electorates would continue in East Pakistan through the election of 1954.

In December, 1906, a group of leading Muslims met in Dhaka at the invitation of Nawab Salimullah of Dhaka and of the Aga Khan. There they founded the All-India Muslim League. The basic goals of the League were to support the Crown and to work for the interests of Muslims in India but not to act against the interests of any other community. The League would have an occasionally rocky path, but it would eventually lead the movement for the partition of India.

The act of 1909 established the elective principle for a portion of the provincial and national legislatures but retained most of the power in the hands of the governors and the officials. Indians began to enter the latter group as members of the Indian Civil Service; Bengali Hindus were well represented but the Muslims of the province were not. In education they continued to lag behind the Hindus.

The act of 1919 (also called the Montagu-Chelmsford Act after the secretary of state and viceroy) expanded the Indian membership of the legislatures and set up a system of "dyarchy" at the provincial level. Under this system, the departments (ministries) that

were related to development, such as education, health, agriculture
and public works, were placed under ministers who were responsible
to the legislature. Departments that served the steel-frame method
of rule (home, finance and revenue) were headed by executive
councilors who were appointed by and responsible to the governor.
Several Bengali Muslims gained important experience during the period of dyarchy by serving as ministers. These included Fazlul Haq
and Khwaja Nazimuddin.

The Muslim League in Bengal became more and more dominated
by a group that would later be called the "national elite." This
group was concerned primarily with the problems of Muslims on the
broad canvas of India as a whole. Many of the group were descendants of Delhi sultanate and Mughal empire officials and used Urdu
as a family language. Nazimuddin (a member of the family of the
Nawab of Dhaka) and the younger Husain Shahid Suhrawardy were
among these, although the latter would later change his course. On
the other hand, there were those of the "vernacular elite," indi-
viduals whose primary concern was the improvement of the status
of the largely impoverished Muslims of Bengal, notably in the eastern
region. They worked in Bengali rather than Urdu. Chief among
these was Fazlul Haq, who prior to the 1937 election would form the
Krishak Praja Party (KPP, farmers', people's party) to oppose the
Muslim League in the Muslim seats and try, with little success, to
enlist peasants from the Hindu community as well. Haq's platform
was based on economic and social issues, the League's on communal
matters.

The Government of India Act of 1935 confirmed the separate
electorates despite strong opposition from the Indian National Congress
led by Mahatma Gandhi. It also provided for fully responsible ministries in the provinces, although emergency powers were retained
by the governors. Following the election of 1937, a coalition government was formed in Bengal under the prime ministership (this term
was used until independence, after which the title became chief minister) of Fazlul Haq but with support of the Muslim League and its
leader, Nazimuddin.

Fazlul Haq and his fellow Muslim prime ministers from the Punjab and Assam, who were also not from the Muslim League, pledged
their support to the Muslim League and Muhammad Ali Jinnah on national issues with the understanding that provincial matters were to
remain in their hands. This pledge, at Lucknow in 1937, was a boost
to Jinnah as the Muslim League had fared poorly in the 1937 election
especially in the Muslim-majority provinces. Fazlul Haq was also the
author of one of several reports which condemned the behavior of
Congress governments toward Muslims in the Muslim-minority provinces.

On March 23, 1940, in Lahore, the Muslim League passed a
resolution often called the "Pakistan resolution" although the word

Pakistan does not appear in it. The resolution stated that if conditions for Muslims in India, especially in the Muslim-minority provinces, did not improve the Muslims would have no choice but to demand that separate states (plural, sic) would have to be established as homelands for the Muslims of India. Fazlul Haq was among the movers of the resolution. The acronym PAKISTAN it should be noted does not contain a letter for Bengal; all of the letters are derived from the northwest of India, present day Pakistan. Fazlul Haq broke with Jinnah in 1941 over the former's membership in the viceroy's war advisory council. Haq resigned from the council but also from the League. The League withdrew its support from Haq's ministry but he was able to continue until 1943 with Hindu assistance. In 1943, Nazimuddin set up a Muslim League ministry which fell in early 1945, and was followed by a short period of governor's rule.

In the 1945 election, Bengali Muslims voted overwhelmingly for the Muslim League, although Fazlul Haq was able to retain his own seat. Among Muslims, the League received 82 percent of the votes, the highest of any of the Muslim-majority provinces. Nazimuddin was not selected again as prime minister. The position went to Suhrawardy. With his support, a meeting of Muslim legislators in New Delhi in 1945 decided that a single state of Pakistan should be formed rather than the two states contemplated in the Lahore resolution.

Suhrawardy waffled later and with some Hindus worked for the creation of a separate "united" Bengal as a third dominion on the subcontinent. He was prime minister during the Great Calcutta Killing in August 1946, but later worked with Gandhi to pacify the city as partition and independence approached. With almost undue haste the new viceroy, Lord Mountbatten, worked toward the end of British rule. This came on August 15, 1947--and the problems of Bengal would continue.

The Pakistan Period

The first independence day of the people of Bangladesh found them as residents of a province, East Bengal, of the Dominion of Pakistan. Jinnah and the central leaders, angered at Suhrawardy's brief espousal of a united Bengal, managed his ouster from the prime ministership and replaced him with Nazimuddin, who became chief minister.

The boundaries of the new province were settled in two ways. The Assamese district of Sylhet contained a majority of Muslims. A plebiscite at the level of subdivision was held there and most of the district voted to join Pakistan. For the division of Bengal itself, a commission headed by a British judge was appointed to determine the contiguous areas of Muslim majority. Some latitude was allowed and the final boundary did not follow precisely the contiguous area formula, but a boundary was established which was workable with one major exception. The land boundary between the West Bengal district of Cooch Behar and the adjoining areas of Bangladesh remains in dispute.

It took little time for the disputes with West Pakistan that would lead to dissolution of united Pakistan to appear. Before the political history is resumed, it is best to look at these grievances.

The government in Karachi seemed to Bengalis to be dominated by persons whose political activity had been either in the areas that remained in India (including Jinnah and the prime minister, Liaqat Ali Khan) or in the provinces included in West Pakistan. Originally only one Bengali, a scheduled caste Hindu, was included in the nine-member cabinet, although he was shortly joined by Khwaja Shahabuddin, a younger brother of Nazimuddin. These choices were clearly not from the vernacular elite. In that group, Fazlul Haq was relegated to the post of advocate general and Suhrawardy, who would soon join the group, remained in India temporarily avoiding the wrath of Jinnah. With Jinnah's death in September 1948, Nazimuddin was appointed governor general but clearly with much less influence than Jinnah. Later another person with remote connections with Bengal, Iskandar Mirza, would become in 1955 the last governor general and in 1956 the first president of Pakistan. His connection, however, was with the family of Sirajuddaulah and Mir Jafar, the latter, of course, not held in high esteem.

It was not only in the political positions in government that the Bengalis had grievances. There were very few Muslim Bengalis in the higher civil service under the British. Consequently, few were taken into the central administration and many posts in the East Bengal provincial administration were filled by Muslims from India or West Pakistan or by rehired British officers. Pakistan would make arrangements through preferences and quotas to attempt to redress the imbalance but these did not result in equality by 1971.

This imbalance was even greater in the military. As already noted, the British had practiced the doctrine of the martial races which all but excluded Bengalis from military service. The practice, however, was continued by the independent Pakistan government: recruits still were very largely drawn from the Punjab and some districts of the NWFP. An answer often given by West Pakistanis to the problem was that there was indeed no martial tradition in Bengal and there were few applicants for military positions. At the time of Bangladeshi independence there were but two Bengalis of general officer rank in the army.

Economic development in the newly independent Pakistan was also uneven. The lack of natural resources in East Bengal made the region a less attractive place for investment than the Punjab and the Karachi area of the west wing. Furthermore, the foreign exchange earnings gained from the export of east wing jute was often invested in the west wing. Moreover, such investment as occurred in the east wing was usually from industrialists based in West Pakistan and this often resulted in an outflow of funds as profits moved to the west wing. For example, the largest jute mill in the world, located in Narayanganj near Dhaka, was owned by a Karachi-based firm, the Adamjees. When, in the 1960s, a study was done of the major industrial and financial groups in Pakistan only, one of these was owned by a native Bengali family, the A. K. Khan group of Chittagong, with investments mainly in textiles and jute. Those in the east wing of Pakistan felt that their agreement to parity in government and in the legislature (see below) would be accompanied by parity in economic development. It must be said that the central government did make efforts to expand the economy of the east wing, but while the East Pakistani economy grew, it grew at a lower rate than that of West Pakistan and the gap increased rather than narrowed.

The issues that have been mentioned were important, but the one that aroused the highest emotional response was that of language. Jinnah and the other key persons in the government had determined that Urdu would be the national language of Pakistan. This decision was taken in spite of Bengali being the language spoken by the majority of the people of Pakistan. Urdu is, furthermore, a language which is not native to Pakistan, its literary home being in Uttar Pradesh and Delhi in India. In addition, many of the contributors to the rich literary heritage of Urdu have been Hindus and Sikhs.

Jinnah, in March 1948, on his only visit to East Bengal after independence, declared that anyone opposing Urdu as the national language was an "enemy" of Pakistan. His views were supported by the chief minister, Nazimuddin, but were widely rejected by the Bengalis. The eventual downfall of the Muslim League can, in large measure, be attributed to the position of Nazimuddin and his ministry. The agitation continued and culminated in the demonstrations held in Dhaka in February 1952. On Febrary 21, several students were killed by the police. The day is still remembered as Martyrs' Day in Bangladesh. Eventually, in September 1954, the constituent assembly of Pakistan decided that "Urdu and Bengali and such other languages as may be declared" shall be the "official languages of the Republic." They added that English would also be used as long as necessary.

Although the language issue was decided in a manner acceptable to the Bengalis, it and the other grievances left a record that would fester and grow into the autonomy and then independence movements that would destroy the unity of Pakistan.

Pakistan took an inordinately long time in framing its constitution, being governed in the meantime by the Government of India Act of 1935 as amended by the India Independence Act of 1947. These

were acts which continued and preserved a viceregal form of government, one in which the governor general would have ultimate power
as the viceroy had before 1947. That is, this would be the system
unless the governor general were a Bengali. During Nazimuddin's
tenure (1948-1951), the locus of power moved to the prime minister,
Liaqat Ali Khan. When Liaqat was assassinated in 1951, Nazimuddin
stepped down from the governor generalship to become prime minister himself. The new governor general, Ghulam Muhammad, a civil
servant before independence, dismissed Nazimuddin in 1953 without
permitting the prime minister to test his support in the constituent
assembly. Other Bengalis (Muhammad Ali Bogra, 1953-1955, and
Suhrawardy, 1956-1957) would be prime ministers but their power
was subject to the whim of the governor general.

A constitution for Pakistan was finally passed and became effective on March 23, 1956. However, it required the Bengalis to
sacrifice their numerical majority in the population and agree to parity in the national parliament. There would be 300 members, 150
from each wing of Pakistan. The votes of Bengalis therefore counted
for less than the votes of West Pakistanis. In an act passed prior
to the constitution, West Pakistan (a term we have been using) was
formally created by the merger of the provinces in the west wing.
(The name of the east wing was changed from East Bengal to East
Pakistan at the same time.) Two provinces with equality in the
parliament was the outcome of these actions. Bengal, led by Suhrawardy, was willing at the time to pay that price if similar parity
could be achieved in other areas, including economic development and
government employment. They were to be disappointed.

Before the constitution was passed, an election had been held
in East Bengal. The position on the language issue was one factor
in the growing discontent with the Muslim League. In 1949, Suhrawardy, returning from India, launched a new political party which
would become the Awami League. It was to be a noncommunal party
open to all residents of Pakistan. Meanwhile, Fazlul Haq had revived his earlier party under a slightly different name, the Krishak
Sramik Party (KSP, peasants' and workers' party, but non-Marxist
unlike some other parties that have used a similar name). These two
parties represented the vernacular elite. They decided to contest
the 1954 election to the East Bengal legislative assembly as a United
Front. The Muslim League was trounced; even Chief Minister Nurul
Amin lost his seat.

The 21-point platform of the United Front was directed largely
at provincial issues. A key matter was the recognition of Bengali
as a national language of Pakistan. Foreshadowing the later Six-
Point Program of Mujibur Rahman was a demand for provincial autonomy except in matters of foreign affairs, defense and currency.
There were also points regarding free trade with and travel to India,
a newly and directly elected constituent assembly, and freedom of
trade in jute.

Suhrawardy directed his attention to national affairs. He departed for Karachi and joined the cabinet of the then prime minister, Muhammad Ali Bogra, also from East Bengal, but a Muslim Leaguer. Suhrawardy became prime minister in 1956. He had key lieutenants in Dhaka, notably Ataur Rahman Khan, who eventually became chief minister, and Sheikh Mujibur Rahman, the key party organizer. He also associated with Maulana Abdul Hamid Khan Bhashani, a leftist religious leader with whom he would split in 1957. Fazlul Haq and his KSP tended to look more toward the provincial arena. He became chief minister briefly in 1954, but the central government intervened and there was a period of governor's rule. Haq had made some remarks during a visit to Calcutta that were interpreted by Karachi as being treasonous in the sense that Haq referred generally to the unity of Bengalis.

By the time parliamentary government was restored in East Pakistan in 1956, the United Front had split and the KSP held a slight edge in the provincial assembly. KSP leader Abu Husain Sarkar became chief minister. Fazlul Haq was named governor. The next two years saw the provincial assembly serve as a battleground between the Awami League and the KSP for control of the East Pakistan government. In 1956 Ataur Rahman Khan became chief minister over the opposition of Governor Fazlul Haq but with the support of the central government now headed by Prime Minister Suhrawardy. By 1958, the tussle became more complicated with a split in the Awami League (see below) and changes in both the governorship and the prime ministership. As Pakistan moved toward military intervention, both Sarkar and Abdur Rahman Khan held the chief ministership in 1958. Turmoil on the streets moved into the assembly house itself to the extent that the deputy speaker died as the result of wounds received on the floor of the assembly.

Meanwhile, as noted earlier, the language issue had been settled, West Pakistan had been unified, and a constitution had become effective on March 23, 1956. It was expected that elections would be held in 1958. Here again, the differences between East and West Pakistan were evident. West Pakistan plumped for the continuance of separate electorates (which Pakistan under Zia ul-Haq has reinstated) on the grounds that these would reinforce the Two Nation Theory. East Pakistan, and here the Awami League and the KSP agreed, favored joint electorates in which there would be no distinction among communities. Their reasoning was fairly straightforward: Muslim votes might be split, but Hindus (then about 20 percent of East Pakistan) would surely not vote for the Muslim League, a party they were not even permitted to join, and would therefore be likely to support one of the members of the United Front ensuring victory for the front. It was decided in Karachi that each province could frame its own election law. It mattered little, for the elections were not held.

It has been mentioned earlier that Suhrawardy and Bhashani

split. Bhashani disagreed with what he believed was a pro-West and pro-market economy stance by Suhrawardy. Bhashani withdrew from the Awami League in 1957 to form the National Awami Party with his followers and with some groups from West Pakistan. Several members of the provincial assembly followed him and these would hold the balance in that body (as they did also in West Pakistan). The jockeying between Sarkar and Abdur Rahman Khan was complicated by the presence of this small but critical group.

On October 7, 1958, President Mirza dismissed the parliament and the two provincial assemblies and the cabinets of Firoz Khan Noon at the center and those in the provinces and proclaimed martial law. Named as chief martial law administrator was General Muhammad Ayub Khan, the army commander-in-chief. On October 28, Ayub dismissed Mirza and assumed the presidency himself.

Although the ending of the parliamentary era was initially welcomed as a relief from the tumultuous politics preceding martial law, it soon became a burden for East Pakistan. Many key oppositionists, including Suhrawardy, Mujib and Fazlul Haq were deprived of their political rights or were jailed. Suhrawardy died in 1963 and the leadership of the Awami League in East Pakistan was taken by Mujibur Rahman. Ataur Rahman Khan eventually left the Awami League to form a splinter party. Fazlul Haq died in 1962 and his party has not since been a factor in East Pakistan or Bangladesh. Nazimuddin returned to politics to lead the Council Muslim League (CML) and the Combined Opposition Parties (COP) group, but he died in 1964. The COP opposed Ayub's reelection in 1965, nominating Jinnah's sister, Fatima, but Ayub won handily in West Pakistan and by a small majority in East Pakistan.

Ayub's newly proclaimed constitution of 1962 changed the electoral system. His form of local government, basic democracy, was based on earlier systems in that locally and directly elected members of the councils were given local administrative and development duties. The new element was that the union councilors would also serve as members of an electoral college for election of the president and the members of the national and provincial assemblies. There were 80,000 councilors, 40,000 in each province. It was clearly easier to control such a small number. The electoral college function came under constant attack from the opposition who favored a system of direct elections by the entire electorate at all levels of government.

Ayub also envisaged a system which would be nonparty. The first elections in 1962 to the national and provincial assemblies were held on this basis. But no sooner had the assemblies convened than parties were formed in them. Ayub, yielding to the inevitable, then convened a session of a party which would support him. This party became the Pakistan Muslim League (Convention). Other Muslim Leaguers formed an opposition group, the Council Muslim League (CML). Still other parties began to function again including, in

East Pakistan, the Awami League led by Mujib and the National
Awami Party led by Bhashani.

After his reelection in 1965, Ayub's stock began to fall for a
number of reasons. Bengalis objected to the war with India in 1965
over Kashmir as, in their view, it left East Pakistan defenseless.
The economy also turned downward and Ayub's health deteriorated.
The upshot was a strong opposition move against him spearheaded
by the newly formed People's Party of Pakistan (PPP) headed by
Zulfiqar Ali Bhutto in West Pakistan and the Awami League in East
Pakistan.

In early 1966, Mujib had proclaimed a platform of six points.
These were (1) a federal government, parliamentary in form, with
free and regular elections; (2) federal government control over only
foreign affairs and defense; (3) a separate currency or separate
accounts for each wing to prevent the movement of capital from the
east to the west; (4) taxation only at the provincial level with
grants from the provinces to support the federal government; (5)
the right of each province to enter into international trade agreements on its own initiative; and (6) each province would raise a
militia. The key provision was not the last but the fourth: without
a source of revenue under its own control the federal government
would be subject to the whim of either provincial government.

In the face of increasing demonstrations, Ayub resigned on
March 25, 1969, and turned the government over to the commander-
in-chief of the army, General Agha Muhammad Yahya Khan, who proclaimed martial law. Yahya promised to hold elections and did so in
December 1970. The election rules for the national assembly scrapped
both the system of separate electorates and the system of parity:
Of the 300 directly elected seats, East Pakistan would have 162 and
West Pakistan 138. The result displayed the polarity between the
two wings. In East Pakistan, the Awami League won 160 of the 162;
in West Pakistan, the PPP won 81 of 138. Neither party won seats
in the other wing.

Yahya opened talks with both Bhutto and Mujib with a view
toward forming a government agreeable to each and toward cooperation in the framing of a new constitution. With mounting pressure
from his supporters, Mujib was forced to stand firmly on the Six
Points as a basis for the constitution. This was adamantly opposed
by both Yahya and Bhutto. Violent demonstrations began in East
Pakistan. At the same time, Yahya increased greatly the number of
troops (almost all of West Pakistani origin) in the east wing. No
agreement was possible. Yahya ordered the troops into action against
the Bengalis on March 25, 1971. Mujib was arrested and taken to
West Pakistan, many Bengalis were killed in the initial assaults and
other Bengalis fled to regroup in India to become the government in
exile and the Mukti Bahini (the national army). India provided a
haven and supplies and entered the war directly in late November.

On December 16, Dhaka fell to the Indians and Bangladesh became independent.

Independent Bangladesh

Bhutto, who had been given power in Pakistan by Yahya, freed Mujib and he returned to a war-weary and badly damaged, but independent, Bangladesh on January 10, 1972. He became prime minister in an Awami League government. A constitution based on a parliamentary system became effective on December 16, 1972. It also enshrined the four principles of Mujibbad (Mujibism): nationalism, secularism, democracy and socialism.

Mujib's associates in the cabinet had little experience in governing; they had been oppositionists during the 13 years of Ayub and Yahya. The transposition was not an easy task. Furthermore, the Bengali members of the Civil Service of Pakistan were often viewed almost as enemies during that period. Some had quickly joined the exile government, many had remained at their posts in Dhaka, and some were posted in West Pakistan and were interned. The military saw a similar division although very few stayed at Pakistani posts in East Pakistan. Yet the work of government required personnel. Many were brought into the administration who had not taken or passed the entrance examinations; many of these were failures. When repatriation of those detained in Pakistan took place in 1973, there was hesitation on the part of the Mujib government about reinstating them in the civil or military services. Bangladesh therefore suffered from poor administration as well as the vast problems of reconstruction and the food shortages which peaked in 1974.

Opposition to Mujib began to increase as the problems mounted. Rapid nationalization of much industry caused severe set backs in production. Corruption became a common occurrence. Although the Awami League won widely in the parliamentary election held in 1973 (292 of 300 directly elected seats), this did not confer legitimacy on what was seen by many as a failing and inefficient government.

To meet the criticism, Mujib drew back from one of his pillars, democracy. On January 25, 1975, the constitution was amended to create a presidential system with Mujib as president and almost all power in his hands. On June 6, 1975, Bangladesh became a one-party state with the Mujib-led Bangladesh Krishak Sramik Awami League (BAKSAL) as the sole legal political grouping. The name combined the heritage of Fazlul Haq and Suhrawardy.

On August 15, 1975, a group of army officers, mostly majors, assassinated Mujib and much of his family (a daughter, Sheikh Hasina Wajid, was in India and escaped, to lead the Awami League later, see below). The majors chose a member of Mujib's cabinet, Khondakar Mushtaque Ahmad, to be president. Mushtaque promised new elections, abolished BAKSAL, and said he would work to restore democracy and faith in the government. However, he remained very much the tool of the majors.

The three days of November 3-5, 1975, were ones of utter confusion in Dhaka. A rebellion took place under the leadership of Brigadier Khalid Musharif who pledged to restore Mujibism. This uprising was put down by the main units of the army, many of whom supported Major General Ziaur Rahman (Zia). Mushtaque resigned, was asked to return, but refused. Chief Justice A.S.M. Sayem became president and chief martial law administrator (CMLA). The key and rising person was Zia.

Zia became CMLA on November 30, 1976, while Sayem remained president. Sayem resigned on grounds of ill health and Zia became president on April 21, 1977. He shortly, on May 30, held a referendum on his continuance in office and, although he gained overwhelming approval, it did not gain legitimacy for him in that no alternative was presented. Having announced a new program (see below), he held a contested election on June 3, 1978. The major contenders were two who had played key roles in the civil war: Zia had commanded a unit of the Mukti Bahini and had, in fact, declared the independence of Bangladesh on March 28, 1971; his opponent, General M. A. G. Osmany, a retired Pakistani officer (as a colonel) had been the commander of the Mukti Bahini and later minister of defense. Zia was backed by the newly formed Jatiyo Ganotantrik Dal (JAGODAL, the National Democratic Party); Osmany by a coalition among which the Awami League was most prominent. Zia's party was formally led by Justice Abdus Sattar, who was appointed vice-president on the day of the election. Zia won with 76.7 percent of the vote to Osmany's 21.7 percent, the balance going to minor candidates.

Zia, looked upon as almost a fish out of water when he first gained power, developed into a charismatic leader. He travelled extensively preaching his program of self-reliance to get Bangladesh moving in development. The key aspects of his Nineteen-Point Program were increased food production and family planning, goals which have been important for President H. M. Ershad as well. Zia began to open up the political system and to curtail the socialist program of the Mujib period. A parliamentary election was held in February 1979. Zia's party, expanded and renamed as the Bangladesh Jatiyatibadi Party (Bangladesh Nationalist Party--BNP) won 207 of the 300 seats in a poll generally judged as fair. The larger faction of a then divided Awami League won 39 seats and the revived Muslim League, 20. Mashiur Rahman, who had been expected to become prime minister, died suddenly and the post was given to Shah Azizur Rahman.

There were other accomplishments and some failures of the Zia regime. Among the former was his championing of the concept of

cooperation among the countries of South Asia. He visited the other
countries in the region and eventually, after his death, seven countries (the others being India, Pakistan, Sri Lanka, Nepal, Bhutan
and the Maldives) agreed in August 1983, in New Delhi to form what
is today called the South Asian Association for Regional Cooperation
(SAARC). A summit meeting in Dhaka in December 1985, ratified
the formation of SAARC. Another summit has been held in Bangalore,
India, and a permanent secretariat has been established in Kathmandu,
Nepal.

On the other hand, Zia failed to establish his system firmly.
It was dependent on him. When he was assassinated on May 30,
1981, he was succeeded by the vice-president, Abdus Sattar, temporarily. The constitution required a new election. Infighting in
the BNP did not permit the choice of a younger candidate. Sattar
ran in the November 15, 1981, election and won, defeating his principal opponent, Kamal Hossain of the Awami League, by a margin of
65.5 percent to 26.0 percent.

Sattar's term turned out to be only an interlude. He was
challenged by the army chief of staff, Husain Muhammad Ershad, who
took deserved credit for quelling the insurrection in which Zia was
assassinated. Ershad called for the cleaning up of the corruption
that undoubtedly existed, but, more importantly, demanded a regu-
larized role for the military in the governance of the country. He
asked specifically for a national security council which would be
dominated by the military. Sattar did reshuffle his cabinet but refused to accept the council. Ershad overthrew Sattar on March 24,
1982.

Ershad's martial law period was not as successful as Zia's in
returning the country to some type of representative government.
He did not assume the presidency until December 11, 1983. He also
used the referendum pattern to gain support for himself and his
program. He won what was reported to be a huge majority in the
March 1985 poll, but most observers felt that the voting was rigged.
His opposition clustered in three groups. The largest was a coalition
led by the Awami League headed by Sheikh Hasina Wajid (a daughter
of Sheikh Mujibur Rahman). A smaller group coalesced around the
BNP led by Khaleda Zia, the widow of Ziaur Rahman. Much less important was a cluster around former president Mushtaque Ahmad.
Ershad made a number of concessions and finally was able to convince
the Awami League-led coalition to contest elections in which it and
Ershad's party, the Jatiyo Dal, were the major contenders. The May
1986 election resulted in a slim majority of the 300 seats for the Jatiyo Dal, with about 100 seats going to the Awami League and its
allies. There were many reports of rigging and some switching of
parties by winners so that the final party totals remained in some
doubt. The BNP-led group boycotted the election.

Parliament first met briefly to hustle through a bill which would grant immunity to Ershad and his government for any acts taken during martial law. Hasina and her group boycotted the session. In the fall of 1986, she officially became leader of the opposition and began to participate, but the going has been rocky and a parliamentary system, even one with major powers retained by the president, is far from an established and going concern in Bangladesh.

Ershad has revamped the local government system, elevating the former subdivisions to the status of districts in a move intended to gain greater popular participation in development. His proposal to include military personnel in the councils was scuttled in the summer of 1987 by wide-scale demonstrations. Ershad has not had and does not have the charisma of Zia as he tries to accomplish his goals. His general development plan, however, is similar in that it emphasizes food production, family planning and health delivery. He also has taken firmer steps to open the economy, including denationalization of some industries and banking institutions.

THE DICTIONARY

ABBASUDDIN AHMAD (1901-1959). A disciple of Kazi Nazrul Islam
(q.v.), spent about 20 years with him. He was a master of at
least two varieties of folk songs--"bhawiya," and "palligeeti."
He influenced the resurgence of Bengali Muslims. He is credited
with having popularized Islamic songs. He is also known for
using a two-string musical instrument (duo tara). He received
the Pride of Performance award from the Pakistan government.
His autobiography is entitled Amar Shilpa Jeban.

ABDUL LATIF, NAWAB (1828-1893). A leading Muslim intellectual
figure in Calcutta in the 19th century, a period when Muslims
lagged well behind Hindus in education. He was an educationist,
author and later prime minister of the princely state of Bhopal
in Central India.

ABDUR RAHIM, SIR (1867-1952). A prominent Muslim Bengali po-
litical figure. He received a legal education in England and re-
turned to India in 1890. He was a founding member of the Mus-
lim League (q.v.). He was elected president of the Central
Legislative Assembly in 1934. Earlier he had been a justice of
the Calcutta High Court and would later be chief justice of
Madras. In addition, he served as Tagore professor of law at
Calcutta University and wrote the authoritative Principles of
Muslim Jurisprudence. His daughter was the first wife of Husain
Shahid Suhrawardy (q.v.).

ABU TAHER, COLONEL (1938-1976). Awarded Bir Uttam for bravery
during the war of liberation, and was executed during the regime of President Ziaur Rahman (q.v.) for his radical leftist beliefs and alleged treason. He joined Jatiya Samajtantrik Dal
(q.v.) in 1974 and introduced to the party the concept of a
people's army. He was a major power broker during the coup
and countercoup of August-November of 1975 but later lost out
to Ziaur Rahman (q.v.). He joined the Pakistan army in 1960
and served in the Special Services group. He was decorated
for his bravery during the Indo-Pakistan war of 1965. After
the Pakistan army crackdown on the civilian population in East
Pakistan, he escaped from West Pakistan to join the war of liberation. He was the first adjutant general of the Bangladesh army.

ABUL HASHIM (1905-1974). A member of the Bengal Assembly (1937-
1947). He joined the Muslim League in 1937 and became general
secretary of the provincial Muslim League in 1943. After the independence of Pakistan he remained in India until 1950 and was
the leader of the opposition in the West Bengal Assembly. For
his role as the president of the organizing committee of the language movement, he was arrested and was jailed for a period
of 16 months. In 1954 he formed the Khilafat-e-Rabbani Party
and was its president till 1956. He was the first director of the
Islamic Academy. He was opposed to the government of President
Ayub Khan.

ABUL HUSAIN (1896-1938). Founder of the Dhaka Muslim Literature
Society in 1923, he was one of the main proponents of the "freedom of thought" movement. He was involved with the education
of the Muslims of Bengal. A liberal thinker, he wrote a number
of books including the Helots of Bengal, Religion of the Helots
of Bengal and the Development of Muslim Law in British India.

ADAMJEE JUTE MILL. Located in Narayanganj in greater Dhaka, is
the largest such mill in the world. It symbolized the domination
of East Pakistani industry by West Pakistanis as the Adamjee family was based in Karachi. In 1954 it was the scene of a major
and violent labor dispute resulting from hiring practices that
seemed to Bengali-speakers to discriminate against them and in
favor of Urdu-speaking Biharis (q.v.). The strike contributed
to the fall of the chief minister, Fazlul Haq (q.v.), and some
have alleged it was intended to do so.

AFGHANISTAN. Bangladesh-Afghanistan relations were not close but
were friendly prior to the communist takeover in Afghanistan in
1978. Since the Soviet invasion of Afghanistan in 1979, the
government of Bangladesh has taken a position similar to that
of Pakistan and most other Islamic nations: the complete withdrawal of Soviet troops, the restoration of the non-aligned position of Afghanistan, and the establishment of a government in
Afghanistan acceptable to the Afghan people. It thus agrees
with and supports the position of Pakistan and opposes the position of India.

AGA KHAN III (Sir Sultan Muhammad Shah, 1877-1957). The spiritual leader of the Nizari Ismaili sect of Shia Muslims. He also
played an important role in Indian-Muslim politics as leader of
the Simla delegation to Lord Minto (q.v.) in 1906 and the founding of the Muslim League (q.v.) in the same year. He was several times president of the Muslim League.

AGARTALA CONSPIRACY CASE. Lodged against Sheikh Mujibur
Rahman (q.v.) and others in 1968. It was alleged that Mujib
and the others had plotted (in the Indian city of Agartala, the
capital of Tripura state) with India to win the independence of
East Pakistan. The trial was never completed and the charges

were dropped by Ayub Khan (q.v.) as a precondition placed by opposition leaders to meetings held between them and Ayub in early 1969.

AGRICULTURE. Agriculture is the largest element in the gross domestic product of Bangladesh accounting for 47.0 percent of the GDP in 1984-85. This can be further divided into crops (36.3 percent), forestry (2.8 percent), livestock (4.9 percent), and fisheries (3.0 percent) of total GDP. The Bangladesh Statistical Yearbook for 1984-85, from which these data are taken, reported that 58.6 percent of persons employed in civilian occupations were engaged in agriculture.

The principal food crop is rice, production of which has increased markedly since independence. On a base year of 1972-73, rice output has increased by 54 percent by 1983-84. Production in the latter year was 14.3 million tons. The major cash and export crop is jute. Production (and the export of raw jute and manufactured products) has declined as the demand for this fiber has declined in the face of competition from synthetic fibers. On the same base of 1972-73, jute output had declined by 20 percent to a production of 931 tons in 1983-84. Tea production, mainly in Sylhet region, had increased sharply (by 23 percent in the same time frame) and is also an important export. However, the quality of Bangladeshi tea in relation to such competitors as India and Sri Lanka is generally rated lower.

Much of the land in Bangladesh is double- or triple-cropped; on the average each acre of cultivated land produced 1.5 crops per year. Of the total cropped area in 1983-84, 7.1 percent was triple-cropped and 39.0 percent double-cropped.

About 12 percent of the land is irrigated by several methods, including deep tubewells, shallow wells, and canals. From the same base year used above, the use of chemical fertilizers had increased by more than 2.5 times by 1983-84. There had been a commensurate increase in the use of pesticides. Nonetheless, agriculture in Bangladesh remains a sector of low yields in comparison with rice growers further east in Asia and one which is very much subject to the vagaries of weather and water supply. For example, in 1988, Bangladesh suffered its worst floods in this century, causing a sharp drop in agricultural production.

AHMAD, ABUL MANSUR (1897-1979). A journalist and a politician. He was the editor of the Daily Ittehad, 1945-1950. In the 1920s he participated in both the Khilafat and the Non-Cooperation movement. He first joined the Swaraj party, then the Congress Party, and finally in 1944 he joined the Muslim League (q.v.). In 1954 he became the minister of health in the United Front (q.v.) government. He was the education and commerce minister when the Awami League (q.v.) was in power in 1956. From 1958 to 1962 he was under arrest. After his release in 1962 he did not return to politics but became a well-known columnist, writing for such papers as Ittefaq and Observer. He wrote a number of books in Bengali.

AHMAD, MUZAFFAR (d. 1972). The leader of the pro-Soviet faction of the National Awami Party (q.v.). He was one of the first political leaders to ask for elections after the independence of Bangladesh. He argued that the 1970 election through which the Awami League (q.v.) came to power was held under conditions prior to independence and the mandate required reconfirmation.

AHMAD, SULTANUDDIN (1902-1977). Governor of East Pakistan in 1958. A lawyer and pre-independence legislator, he also served as ambassador of Pakistan in Burma, China and Indonesia.

AHMAD, TAJUDDIN (1922-1975). Headed the first provisional government of Bangladesh. He was a close confidant of Sheikh Mujibur Rahman (q.v.) during negotiation with both the Ayub (q.v.) and the Yahya (q.v.) regimes. Preferring closer ties with the Soviet Union, he fell into disgrace when Mujib felt circumstances required a closer relationship with United States. He was one of the four political leaders who were assassinated following the Khalid Musharif (q.v.) coup of November 1975.

AHMED, MOUDUD (b. 1940). Named prime minister by President Ershad (q.v.) in March 1988. Active in the 1971 liberation movement, he later broke with Mujibur Rahman (q.v.) and worked often as a civil rights lawyer. He held ministerial posts under Ziaur Rahman (q.v.), 1977-1980, and was elected to parliament in 1979. He was appointed to the Ershad cabinet in 1985 and named deputy prime minister in 1986, a post he held until becoming prime minister. He was elected to parliament from Noakhali in 1986 and 1988.

AHSAN-UL-HUQUE (b. 1919). His father, Sir Muhammad Aziz-ul-Huque, (q.v.) was a prominent Muslim Bengali political figure before independence, and he himself engaged principally in commerce and industry. He served as a Pakistan ambassador under Ayub Khan (q.v.) and was a member of the cabinet formed by Yahya Khan (q.v.) in 1969 in the latter's unsuccessful effort toward gradual civilianization of the martial law government.

AKRAM KHAN, MAULANA MUHAMMAD (1868-1968). A founding member of the Muslim League (q.v.) in 1906. He founded the newspaper Danik Azad. He was the president of the provincial Muslim League and vice-president of All-India Muslim League and Pakistan Muslim League. He was also a social activist and a litterateur and was given the Pride of Performance in Literature award by the government of Pakistan.

ALAUDDIN HUSSAIN SHAH. The sultan of Bengal from 1493 to 1518 and the founder of the Sayyid dynasty (q.v.). The dynasty took its name as Alauddin was a Sayyid of Arab descent. He proved to be a very successful and popular ruler.

ALI, MAHMUD (b. 1919). Leader of the Ganotantrik Dal (q.v.), a
constituent of the United Front (q.v.) which swept the 1954
election to the East Bengal Legislative Assembly. After Bangladeshi independence, he chose to move to Pakistan and has held
a variety of posts under both the Bhutto (q.v.) and Zia ul-Haq
regimes.

ALIVARDI KHAN (c. 1676-1756). Became governor of Bengal in
1740. He had been the previous governor's deputy for the Bihar
region of the Bengal province of the Mughals. Taking advantage
of the confusion in Delhi caused by the raid of the Persian Nadir
Shah and with the help of dubious documents, he claimed that
he had been chosen to replace the incumbent governor. His term
in office was relatively peaceful as he successfully met the challenges presented by the British. He was succeeded by his
grandson, Sirajuddaulah (q.v.).

AMIR ALI, SYED (1849-1928). A Bengali Shia, wrote extensively on
Islam. He was the founder of the National Muhammadan Association, a Calcutta-based group for the expression of Muslim political views. He was a judge of the Calcutta High Court, 1890-
1904. He reentered politics after his retirement from the bench.
He was a member of the Simla delegation to Lord Minto (q.v.)
in 1906 and led a Muslim League delegation to Lord Morley in
London in 1909. He was a champion of the cause of separate
electorates.

ASIATIC SOCIETY OF BANGLADESH. An outgrowth of the Asiatic
Society of Bengal, was an association of learned men interested
in oriental studies. It was founded by Sir William Jones in 1784
and supported by Governor General Warren Hastings (q.v.). It
maintains an extensive library of books and manuscripts. In
1951, the Asiatic Society of Pakistan was formed by Dr. M.
Shahidullah (q.v.). When Bangladesh became independent in
1971, the organization was renamed the Asiatic Society of Bangladesh.

ATAUR RAHMAN KHAN (b. 1907). Became a member of the Awami
League at its inception in 1949. He acted as president of the
East Bengal Awami League several times when the head of the
provincial organization, Maulana Bhashani (q.v.), was in jail.
He was elected to the East Bengal Assembly in 1954 and was
leader of the Awami League part of the United Front. After
representative government was restored to the province in 1956,
he served as chief minister of East Pakistan throughout much of
the period from 1956 to 1958 (when Ayub Khan's [q.v.] coup
displaced him), with the exception of short periods when the
Krishak Sramik Party (q.v.) leader Abu Husain Sarkar (q.v.)
was able to form a government.
    After the death of Awami League founder H. S. Suhrawardy
(q.v.) in 1963, his relations with Sheikh Mujibur Rahman (q.v.)

became difficult and in the 1970 election Ataur Rahman Khan
formed the Pakistan (later Bangladesh) National League. He was
defeated in 1970 but won election to the Bangladesh Parliament
in 1973 (and was leader of the opposition in 1975 when Mujibur
Rahman imposed one-party rule) and again in 1979. On March
30, 1984, he was appointed prime minister by the martial law
president, H. M. Ershad (q.v.), and held that office until January 7, 1985, when Ershad reshuffled the entire cabinet.

AUGUST COUP. The first coup by the Bangladesh army took place
on August 15, 1975. This coup led to the assassination of Sheikh
Mujibur Rahman (q.v.) and the collapse of the first democratically elected government of Bangladesh. Welcomed widely by the
people of Bangladesh, the coup was led by junior ranking members of the army including two lieutenant colonels and five majors. The August coup was followed by the November 1975 coup
and countercoup in which Khalid Musharif (q.v.) was killed and
Ziaur Rahman (q.v.) became the key person in government.

AWAMI LEAGUE. Founded in June 1949 as the Awami ("People's")
Muslim League, by Husain Shahid Suhrawardy (q.v.) as a vehicle
for his political ambitions and as a party which would be an alternative to the Muslim League (q.v.). Suhrawardy opposed
the clause in the Muslim League constitution which prohibited
non-Muslims from becoming members, stating that this would
cause continued divisions in Pakistan; hence, the word Muslim
was soon dropped from the new party's name. The party developed little strength in West Pakistan, but emerged as the
strongest party in East Pakistan. It joined with the Krishak
Sramik Party (q.v.) and some smaller parties in the United Front
(q.v.) of 1954, which won the legislative election in East Bengal
from the Muslim League.

Among those closely associated with Suhrawardy were Ataur
Rahman Khan (q.v.), chief minister for most of the period from
1956 to 1958; Sheikh Mujibur Rahman (q.v.), organizational leader
during the same period and after the death of Suhrawardy, de
facto leader of the party; and Maulana Abdul Hamid Khan Bhashani (q.v.).

Bhashani differed with Suhrawardy on domestic and international issues and left the party in 1957 to form the National
Awami Party (q.v.). The program of the party in economic
matters was middle of the road, although after Bangladeshi independence Mujibur Rahman, as prime minister and later as
president, pursued a strong program of nationalization of industry and trade. Before independence, Mujib supported a high degree of autonomy for the provinces of Pakistan; this was embodied
in the Six-Point Program (q.v.) Mujib proclaimed in 1966.

In the 1970 elections the Awami League swept both the East
Pakistan segment of the National Assembly and East Pakistan Provincial Assembly polls. After Bangladeshi independence, the
Awami League held office until mid-1975, when it merged into

BAKSAL (q.v.). After the November 1975 coup and after political parties were permitted to return to activity, the party
was revived. It supported Muhammad Ataul Ghani Osmany (q.v.)
for president in 1978 and participated in the 1979 parliamentary
elections, winning about 10 percent of the seats and becoming
the official opposition to the Bangladesh Nationalist Party (BNP)
(q.v.). In the presidential election in 1981, following the assassination of Ziaur Rahman (q.v.), the Awami League candidate,
Kamal Husain (q.v.) finished second to the BNP's Abdus Sattar
(q.v.). Banned again after the coup led by General H. M.
Ershad (q.v.) in 1982, the party revived once again to finish
second in the 1986 parliamentary elections to Ershad's Jatiyo Dal
(q.v.). The party did not contest the 1986 presidential election
which was won by Ershad. The Awami League favors a West-
minster form of parliamentary government with a secular and
socialist society and economy. The present leader of the party
and leader of the opposition in parliament is Sheikh Hasina Wajid
(q.v.), daughter of Mujibur Rahman.

AYUB KHAN, MUHAMMAD (1907-1974). President of Pakistan, 1958-
1969, was a career military officer in the Indian and Pakistani
armies, having been commissioned from Sandhurst in 1928. He
reached the rank of major general in 1948 while he was in command of the troops stationed in East Bengal. In 1951, having
reached the rank of lieutenant general, he was appointed the
first Pakistani to be commander-in-chief of the army (his pre-
decessors since independence in 1947 had been British officers
seconded to the Pakistani Army). He was additionally minister
of defense in the "cabinet of talents" headed by Muhammad Ali
Bogra (q.v.) from October 1954 to August 1955 and during this
time was a key person in the negotiation of military assistance
from the United States to Pakistan.

In October 1958 he became chief martial law administrator (until 1962) following the dismissal of civilian government by President Iskandar Mirza (q.v.); Ayub then deposed Mirza in the same
month and became president (until 1969). Rioting in opposition
to his rule began in West Pakistan in September 1968 and quickly
spread to East Pakistan. Despite his offer to restore parliamentary
rule and his withdrawal of the Agartala Conspiracy Case (q.v.)
against Mujibur Rahman (q.v.) and others, he was forced by
leaders of the military to resign the presidency to General Agha
Muhammad Yahya Khan (q.v.). While Ayub's period of rule displayed considerable economic growth in East Pakistan, the growth
in West Pakistan was much more rapid, leading to a marked increase in the economic disparity between the two provinces.

AZAM KHAN, MUHAMMAD GENERAL (b. 1901). Appointed the administrator of Martial Law Zone B, which included the whole of West
Pakistan except Karachi, when General Ayub (q.v.) took over in
1958. He was given high credit for his reorganization of the
Ministry of Refugee and Rehabilitation. In 1960 he was appointed

governor of East Pakistan. He became a very popular governor
because of his untiring effort to reach the people. His popu-
larity was seen as a threat to General Ayub who removed him in
1962. He came to prominence once again when he joined the opposition and supported the presidential candidacy of Fatima Jinnah
against Ayub Khan in 1964.

AZIZ-UL-HUQUE, SIR MUHAMMAD (1890-1947). A lawyer by profession, served as a member of the Governor General's Advisory
Council in 1943. Prior to that he was the Indian High Commissioner to England (1941). His effort in the field of education is
well recognized. As Vice-Chancellor of Calcutta University from
1938 to 1942 he established the first Islamic History and Culture
department. He was earlier (1934) an education minister of Bengal. He was a member of the Bengal Provincial Council. Prior
to the independence of Pakistan he was the Legal Advisor to the
government of India. He wrote the book Man Behind the Plough.
His son Ahsan-ul-Huque (q.v.), served in the Pakistan cabinet.

AZIZUR RAHMAN, SHAH MOHAMMAD (1925-1988). Secretary general
of the All-India Muslim Students Federation and All Bengal Muslim
Students League from 1945-1947. He became the joint secretary
of the East Pakistan Muslim League in 1947 and became the general secretary from 1952-1958. He joined the Awami League (q.v.)
in 1964. In 1969 he was the deputy leader of the Pakistan National Assembly. During the war of independence he remained
out of politics and reemerged in politics when the Bangladesh
Muslim League was permitted to operate in 1976. In 1979 he was
elected a member of the parliament and became the prime minister
of the country. He joined the Bangladesh Nationalist Party (q.v.).
He remained as the prime minister until December 1981. After
the assassination of President Ziaur Rahman (q.v.), he remained
with the party until he was expelled from the Bangladesh Nationalist Party in 1985.

- B -

BADRUNNESSA AHMAD (1929-1974). Served as minister of education
in the Sheikh Mujibur Rahman (q.v.) government which was
formed after the parliamentary election of 1973. She was a member of the East Bengal Legislative Assembly from 1954 to 1958.
She served as the vice-president of the Mahila Samity (Women's
Organization) of East Pakistan and later Bangladesh from 1959 to
1972. A member of the Awami League, she actively participated
in the war of liberation by propagating the Bangladeshi cause.
Like many of her contemporaries, she too was arrested during the
language movement (see Martyrs' Day).

BAKSAL. An acronym for Bangladesh Krishak Sramik Awami League,
the name chosen by Sheikh Mujibur Rahman (q.v.) for the single

party in Bangladesh decreed by him in June 1975. The name combined the names of the two of the parties, Awami League (q.v.) and Krishak Sramik Party (q.v.), that had joined to form the United Front (q.v.) in 1954. Not all Awami Leaguers agreed to join the new party; those who did not were technically out of politics. BAKSAL was dissolved following the assassination of Mujibur Rahman on August 15, 1975, and the installation of a new government under Khondakar Mushtaque Ahmad (q.v.).

BANG TRIBE. Believed to have been the first Indo-Aryan group to have migrated to the lower Ganges valley and to have given its name to Bengal. (In Sanskrit, the tribe is Vang and the area Vanga [q.v.]).

BANGLADESH KRISHAK SRAMIK AWAMI LEAGUE see BAKSAL

BANGLADESH MUSLIM LEAGUE. An outgrowth of the Pakistan Muslim League, itself an outgrowth of the Muslim League (q.v.) which was established in 1906. The Pakistan Muslim League was the most popular party in East Pakistan until the provincial election of 1954 when it lost heavily to the Awami League (q.v.). In the 1960s the Pakistan Muslim League broke into two factions: The Pakistan Muslim League (Convention) (q.v.) and the Council Muslim League (q.v.). After the independence of Bangladesh, both factions were banned. These two factions cooperated after the passing of the Political Parties Regulation Act of 1976 and formed the Bangladesh Muslim League. In 1978 this party split into two factions. The more conservative group was led by Khan Abdul Sobur (q.v.) while the more liberal wing was led by Shah Aziaur Rahman (q.v.).

BANGLADESH NATIONALIST PARTY (BNP). Originally formed in 1978 as the political vehicle for the associates of the then president, Ziaur Rahman (q.v.). Zia had been elected in June 1978, as the candidate of JAGODAL (an acronym for the Bengali equivalent of "People's Party"). Beside JAGODAL, the party included elements from the leftist National Awami Party (q.v.), the conservative Bangladesh Muslim League (q.v.) and several other smaller parties and groups. The party supported the Nineteen-Point Program (q.v.). The titular leader of the party was Justice Abdus Sattar (q.v.), who succeeded Ziaur Rahman as president when the latter was assassinated in 1981. The BNP won more than two-thirds of the parliamentary seats in the 1979 elections. After Zia's assassination and the coup which ousted Sattar in 1982, the party has been led by Ziaur Rahman's widow, Khalida Zia. It boycotted the 1986 parliamentary elections. Before and after the elections it saw many key members defect, usually to support President H. M. Ershad (q.v.) and his Jatiyo Dal (q.v.).

BASIC DEMOCRACY. The term used for local government during the

Ayub Khan (q.v.) regime. Insofar as local government itself was concerned it was not a radical change from previous systems. Local (union) councils of 7 to 15 members were elected by direct franchise, each member to represent about 1,000 persons. Parity (q.v.) was applied so that there were 40,000 basic democrats from each wing. Local duties included some powers of taxation, administration, adjudication and development. Higher levels of government were also covered by the system at the tehsil (West Pakistan) and thana (East Pakistan) tiers and at the district. The innovation by Ayub was that the 80,000 basic democrats would also serve as an electoral college for the presidency and the members of the national and provincial assemblies. This last aspect was strongly opposed by the Combined Opposition Parties (q.v.) and other opposition groups. These groups favored a system of direct elections at all levels of government (and, generally, also favored a parliamentary system).

BASIC PRINCIPLES REPORT. The working draft which culminated in the 1956 constitution of Pakistan (q.v.). The report was first published in 1950 and was criticized by the United Front (q.v.) because, among other things, of its proposition that Urdu be the national language of Pakistan.

BAULS. A rustic group of troubadors who travel from one area to another singing devotional songs. They often use a one-string instrument (ektara) for their music. They practice a combination of Islam and Hinduism. They are also known for their long, braided hair which is knotted.

BAYAZID. Son of Sulaiman Karnani, was sultan of Bengal from 1562 to 1572. He succeeded his father, but soon lost Bengal to the Mughal Emperor Akbar in 1576.

BAYAZID BASTAMI. A Persian who was born in the 9th century, settled in Chittagong. He was a preacher and there are numerous myths and legends about him. He converted a large number of Hindus and Buddhists to Islam. His tomb in Chittagong is an important pilgrimage site. The tomb is near a small pond which is known for its numerous large tortoises suggesting that the site may have an older Hindu connection.

BENGAL, PARTITION OF (1905). The then viceroy, Lord Curzon (q.v.), determined that the province of Bengal (which then included approximately the present territory of Bangladesh and the Indian states of West Bengal, Bihar and Orissa) was too large to be administered efficiently. Curzon decreed a partition in 1905. One new province named Eastern Bengal and Assam joined roughly what is Bangladesh today with the area north and northeast of it. It had a Muslim majority. The capital was Dhaka. The other province was named Western Bengal, Bihar and Orissa. It had a Hindu majority, but the Bengalis were no longer the majority

group being outnumbered by the combined Biharis and Oriyas.
The capital was Calcutta. Bengali Hindus objected strongly to
the partition and this was expressed through writing, speeches,
demonstrations, boycotts of British goods, violence and terrorism.
Bengali Muslims were, expectedly, pleased with the prospect of
a province in which they would be a majority especially as new
reforms by the British were expected to include provincial elections. The British finally heeded the Hindu objections and the
partition was annulled in 1911. Bengal was reunited, Assam
separated and Bihar and Orissa joined in a single province (they
were separated in 1919). Accompanying the annulment was the
British decision to transfer the capital of India from Calcutta
to New Delhi.

BENGAL, PARTITION OF (1947). The partition of India in 1947 also
required the partition of two provinces: the Punjab and Bengal.
A commission headed by a British judge, Sir Cyril (later Lord)
Radcliffe, was charged with the task of determining the boundaries. The basic rule was that contiguous areas with Muslim
majorities would go to Pakistan. Some leeway was permitted in
the decision. In dividing Bengal, the commission decided that
Khulna district, despite its Hindu majority, would go to Pakistan
and Murshidabad district, despite its Muslim majority, would go
to India. One reason for the latter decision was that West Bengal would have been split in two parts if a connecting area in
Murshidabad were not given to India. Some other districts, e.g.,
Malda, were divided between the two countries. The Sylhet
Referendum (q.v.) was also held to decide the boundary between
East Bengal and Assam.

BERUBARI ENCLAVE. A small piece of territory which was awarded
to East Bengal in the partition of 1947 (see Bengal, Partition of
[1947]) but is surrounded by Indian territory. Pakistan (and
later, Bangladesh) and India have been unable to sort out the
question of pieces of territory in north Bengal. The enclaves
result primarily from the exclaves of the former princely state
of Cooch Behar.

BHADRALOK. Literally, means respected people or gentlemen. They
are socially privileged, educated members of society who had distinct speech, dress, housing and eating habits. The bhadralok
abstained from manual labor. The term is infrequently used in
Bangladesh, as it is linked primarily to the Hindu caste system.

BHASHANI, MAULANA ABDUL HAMID KHAN (1885-1976). A leader
of the Muslim League (q.v.) in Assam before independence, although originally from Tangail district of eastern Bengal. He
returned to East Bengal after independence and became a founder-
member of the Awami League (q.v.) in 1949 and president of the
East Bengal provincial unit of the party. Although holding the
Islamic title "maulana," he was often viewed as being on the left

in politics, espousing the cause of the peasantry against the holders of power in the villages and, in international affairs, opposing the West and favoring closer ties with China, a product, as he saw it, of a peasant revolution. It was over international issues that he broke with H. S. Suhrawardy (q.v.) in 1956, when Suhrawardy supported Pakistan's growing ties with the United States. He and his associates from the Awami League formed the National Awami Party (q.v.) in 1957, bringing his East Pakistani group into association with the Pakistan National Party of West Pakistan. In East Pakistan and in national politics Bhashani continued to play a prominent role in opposition (except on Ayub Khan's policy of opening relations with China) until his death. He opposed Mujibur Rahman (q.v.), most notably when he led protests against the Indo-Bangladesh treaty (q.v.) in 1972.

BHUTTO, ZULFIQAR ALI (1928-1979). A member of a prominent Sindhi family, began his political career when he was appointed a minister in the first cabinet of Ayub Khan (q.v.) in 1958. He was foreign minister, 1963-1966. Resigning from the cabinet over differences with Ayub Khan on relations with India, he founded the Pakistan Peoples Party (PPP) in 1967 and remained its chairman until his death. The PPP won the majority of seats from West Pakistan in the National Assembly elected in December 1970, but won none in East Pakistan.

In the negotiations following the election, Bhutto maintained that there were two majorities in Pakistan: his in West Pakistan and that of the Awami League (q.v.) led by Mujibur Rahman (q.v.) in East Pakistan. His actions along with those of President Yahya Khan (q.v.) are credited with bringing about the impasse which led to the breakdown of negotiations and the outbreak of civil war in March 1971. With the defeat of the Pakistani forces in December 1971, Yahya Khan resigned and turned the government over to Bhutto and the PPP. Bhutto was president of Pakistan, 1971-1973, and, after a new constitution was adopted, prime minister, 1973-1977. He was overthrown in a coup led by General Muhammad Zia ul-Haq on July 5, 1977. Charged with complicity in a murder, Bhutto was convicted and hanged on April 4, 1979.

BIHARIS. The term used to describe those Muslim refugees from Bihar in 1947 who fled eastward to East Bengal rather than westward to West Pakistan as did most refugees from India. The group is Urdu-speaking and found it difficult to integrate with the Bengali-speakers in whose midst they found themselves. The term may also be derived from baharis (Urdu for "outsiders"). They were and remained strong supporters of the Pakistan idea and many were accused of supporting the Pakistan army in 1971. There were about 600,000 Biharis at that time. After independence, they were often shunned by Bangladeshis and their plight made international news. Since then many have gone to Pakistan, legally or illegally; some remain in camps, and some younger Biharis have integrated into Bangladeshi society.

BISWAS, ABDUL LATIF (1892-1964). A leader of the Krishak Praja Party, was the secretary of the Krishak Sramik Party (q.v.). Between 1926 and 1945 he was a member of the Bengal Legislative Council and the Bengal Legislative Assembly. In 1954, he was the Minister of Land Revenue in the United Front (q.v.) government and became the central minister for Food and Agriculture in 1955. At his death he was a member of the National Democratic Front in opposition to Ayub Khan (q.v.).

BOGRA, MUHAMMAD ALI (of) (1901-1963). A member of a leading landowning family in eastern Bengal. He was elected to the Bengal Legislative Assembly in 1937 and 1946 and was appointed a parliamentary secretary in the Nazimuddin (q.v.) government in 1943 and a minister in 1946. After independence, he held high diplomatic posts (although retaining his membership of the constituent assembly): ambassador to Burma in 1948, high commissioner to Canada in 1949, and ambassador to the United States in 1952. He was summoned back from the latter post to become prime minister in 1953, following the dismissal of Nazimuddin from that post. His first cabinet was political, but he reorganized the cabinet in 1954 to form a "cabinet of talents," including, among others, General Ayub Khan (q.v.). He was dismissed in 1955 and returned to the United States as ambassador, 1955-1958. Inactive in the first part of Ayub's regime, he became minister of foreign affairs in 1962, holding the post until his death.

BOGRA MUTINY. One of the more significant coup attempts during the regime of President Ziaur Rahman (q.v.). An army tank regiment in Bogra attempted to seize the local air force base in order to negotiate the freedom of Lieutenant Colonel Farook Rahman, who was one of the majors who led the first army coup in Bangladesh that led to the assassination of Sheikh Mujibur Rahman (q.v.). This coup started on September 30, 1977, and spread to Dhaka on October 2, 1977. The Dhaka phase of the coup attempt coincided with the hijacking of a Japan Airline aircraft that landed at Dhaka airport. This coup attempt led to 11 Air Force officers' being killed. As a result of the coup attempt a large number of army personnel were executed. Amnesty International protested the summary execution.

BUDDHISM. The small Buddhist population in Bangladesh is concentrated in the Chittagong Hills Tracts (q.v.) or is made up of migrants from the hills. The 1981 census enumerated 538,000 Buddhists, of whom 73.2 percent lived in the hill tracts and 23.0 percent in the neighboring Chittagong region. These Buddhists are almost invariably members of one of the tribal groups (see Tribes) residing in the area. There are no restrictions on employment, private or public, placed on Buddhists and their principal holidays are national or regional holidays.

BULBUL CHOUDHURY (1919-1954). A renowned dancer and writer.
His real name was Rashid Ahmad Choudhury. He first achieved
prominence because of his work in one of Tagore's (q.v.) dance
dramas. In 1937, he founded the Oriental Fine Arts Association
in Calcutta and made original contributions to understanding and
propounding fine arts. During the period 1943-48 he joined the
civil service and worked as a public information officer in the
Ministry of Information. In 1948 he resigned from the service
and founded his own dance group. In 1950 he moved to Dhaka
from Calcutta. Between 1950 and 1952 he visited a number of
European countries performing with his dance group. In 1955
he established the Bulbul Fine Arts Academy, which continues
to be a major center of fine arts in the country. He also wrote
several plays.

BURMA. Burma is the only country other than India (q.v.) to
share a border with Bangladesh. The border was undemarcated
prior to 1985 when an agreement was reached between the two
countries. Relations between the two countries have been at
least correct and generally cordial with the exception of an interlude in 1976. At that time a substantial number (estimated vari-
ously at 100,000) of Muslims from the Arakan region of Burma
fled into Bangladesh, apparently as a result of the application of
a new citizenship law in Burma that would have left the Arakanese
Muslims in a legally subordinate position. Negotiations between
the two countries resulted in the return of the refugees to Burma
and the restoration of cordial relations.

- C -

CABINET MISSION PLAN. Proposed by a three-member team of the
British cabinet that visited India in 1946. Sir Stafford Cripps
was the most prominent member. The plan called for a three-
tier government for a united India in which the powers of the
federal (central) government would be limited to foreign affairs,
defense, currency and communications. All other powers would
devolve to the provinces. The provinces would be grouped in
to three zones: (1) Bengal and Assam (Muslim majority); (2)
the Punjab, the Northwest Frontier Province, Sind and Balchistan
(Muslim majority); and (3) the other provinces (Hindu majority).
The provinces could delegate upward such powers as they chose
to the zonal groupings. Minority rights would be guaranteed.
The Muslim League (q.v.) accepted the plan. The Congress accepted with such reservations that it was taken by the League
to be a rejection. The plan was therefore discarded.

CASTE. Caste is the hereditary and hierarchical division of society
in Hinduism (q.v.). The term is also used loosely in Islam in
the sub-continent despite Islam's being an egalitarian religion.
Probably a holdover from the pre-Islamic period, caste as used

by Muslims is often important in status assignments and in such rites as marriage, especially in rural areas.

CHINA. Initially, relations between China and Bangladesh did not exist on a formal basis as China supported the Pakistani position that Bangladesh was an illegal creation. China exercised its veto in the Security Council to exclude Bangladesh from membership in the United Nations. The recognition of Bangladesh by Pakistan through the good offices of members of the Organization of the Islamic Conference (q.v.) rendered the Chinese position null. China and Bangladesh established diplomatic relations in 1976, following the assumption of power by Ziaur Rahman (q.v.).

Relationships have grown. There have been a number of high-level visits, China has provided limited military and economic assistance and, to a degree, trade has been developed. A contributing factor, no doubt, has been the cooling of relations with India (q.v.) and with the Soviet Union (see Union of Soviet Socialist Republics), coupled with the close Indo-Soviet ties.

CHITTAGONG HILL TRACTS. Located in the southeast corner of Bangladesh and bordering on both India and Burma. The area was set aside by the British as an area for tribal groups including such tribes as the Chakma and Maghs. Under the British, land ownership in the region was not permitted to non-tribals. Since independence there has been some influx of plains people to the Hill Tracts. This has been opposed, often violently, by the tribals and a low level of guerrilla warfare has been endemic to the region. Some land was lost to the tribals through the building of the Karnaphuli hydroelectric station and the ponding of water behind the dam.

CHOUDHURY, A. K. M. FAZLUL QADER (1919-1973). A lawyer by profession, he served the Muslim League in numerous capacities. He joined the party in 1938. He was the general secretary of the All-India Muslim Student Federation. He was an elected member of the East Bengal Legislative Assembly in 1954 and a member of the National Assembly of Pakistan in 1962. A member of the Ayub (q.v.) cabinet in 1962, he later was speaker of the National Assembly, 1963-1966. During the movement to oust President Ayub he remained loyal and was the president of Pakistan Muslim League (Convention). He worked against the liberation of Bangladesh, and for his association with the Razzakar Bahini (q.v.) and the Peace Committees (q.v.), he was arrested after the liberation of Bangladesh. He died while he was in jail.

CHOUDHURY, HAMIDUL HAQ (b. 1903). A lawyer, political figure and newspaper owner (of the former Pakistan Observer, now Bangladesh Observer, published in Dhaka). He was elected to the Bengal Legislative Council in 1937 and to the Legislative

Assembly in 1946, serving as a minister in the Nurul Amin (q.v.) cabinet. He was also elected a member of the constituent assembly in 1946 and 1955. He was foreign minister in 1955 in the cabinet of Chaudhury Muhammad Ali and again in the cabinet of Firoz Khan Noon (q.v.) in 1958. He was banned from politics for seven years under Ayub Khan (q.v.), but was a member of the Democratic Action Committee (q.v.) opposing Ayub in 1969. He opposed the separation of East Pakistan and remained for several years in Karachi, but has since returned to Dhaka and had his properties, including the newspaper, restored to him.

CHOUDHURY, MOAZZAM HUSSAIN (LAL MIA) (1905-1967). Central minister for Health, Labor and Social Welfare in 1965. Prior to that he was the chief whip of the Pakistan Muslim League (q.v.) and member of the National Assembly of Pakistan. Earlier he participated in the Non-Cooperation movement and the Khalifat movement (both in the early 1920s) and was jailed by the British. He joined the Muslim League in 1943. He was also a poet and published two books of poems. He changed his name later to Abdullah Zahiruddin, but was known by the nickname Lal Mia. He was the brother of Yusuf Ali Choudhury (q.v.).

CHOUDHURY, MUNIR (1925-1971). Obtained a Master's degree in Linguistics from Harvard University. He was fluent in English and Bengali and was a faculty member in both Dhaka and Rajshahi universities. In 1943 he formed the Writers Association. He joined the Communist Party in Calcutta in 1948. He actively participated in the language movement to make Bengali one of the national languages of Pakistan and was jailed several times between 1952 and 1955. Some of his major works were written while he was in jail, including the play "Kobor" (grave). He received a number of awards including the Sitara-e-Imtiaz in 1966 which he renounced in 1971. He also developed the Bengali typewriter. He was one of the intellectuals who was murdered by the Pakistani forces.

CHOUDHURY, YUSUF ALI (MOHAN MIA) (1905-1971). A provincial minister in the United Front (q.v.) government. He started his political life as a member of the Faridpur Municipality and later became the Chairman of the Faridpur District Council. He was also a member of the Bengal Legislative Assembly before 1947. He was an active member of the Muslim League (q.v.) serving as the Chairman of the Faridpur district Muslim League and in 1952 became the president of the East Pakistan Muslim League. He was ousted from the Muslim League in 1953. He then joined the Krishak Sramik party (q.v.) of A. K. Fazlul Haq (q.v.) and became its general secretary in 1957. In the 1960s he joined the National Democratic Front and was a member of the National Democratic Movement which was formed to oust the government of Ayub Khan (q.v.). He became a member of a faction of the Muslim League once again in 1969. He was opposed to the freedom

movement of Bangladesh. He started a charity organization
called the Khademul Islam (Servants of Islam) and the paper
Daily Millat. He was the brother of Moazzam Hussain Choudhury
(q.v.).

CHOUDHURY, ZAHUR AHMED (1916-1974). Joined the Awami League
in 1949 and served as its Labor Secretary in 1957. He was
elected to the Bengal Provincial Assembly in 1954, to the East
Pakistan Provincial Assembly in 1970, and to the National Assembly of Bangladesh in 1973. According to the Awami League
version of the declaration of independence of Bangladesh, Zahur
Ahmed Choudhury carried the declaration from Sheikh Mujibur
Rahman (q.v.) and gave it to Ziaur Rahman (q.v.) to be announced over Chittagong radio on March 25, 1971. Instead, according to this version, Zia made the announcement but also
declared himself president of Bangladesh.

CHOWDHURY, ABU SAYEED (1921-1987). President of Bangladesh,
January 1972-December 1973. Earlier he had been a justice of
the Dhaka High Court and a vice-chancellor of Dhaka University.
Out of Pakistan, attending a meeting of the UN Commission on
Human Rights in March 1971, he was able to play a key role as
a roving ambassador in Europe and the United States on behalf
of emerging Bangaldesh. He was briefly foreign minister in 1975,
but thereafter remained out of politics.

CHOWDHURY, ABUL FAZAL MOHAMMAD AHSANUDDIN (b. 1915).
Appointed president of Bangladesh by H. M. Ershad (q.v.) in
March 1982. He resigned the office in December 1984, when
Ershad himself assumed the presidency. Earlier he had been a
jurist, retiring from the Supreme Court in 1977.

CHOWDHURY, MIZANUR RAHMAN (b. 1931). Prime minister of
Bangladesh under President Ershad (q.v.), was a member of the
Pakistan National Assembly from 1962 to 1969. He was for a
time the Acting General Secretary of the East Pakistan Awami
League. During the movement to oust the regime of President
Ayub Khan (q.v.) he was one of the organizers of the Combined
Opposition Parties (q.v.). He was elected twice to the Bangladesh
National Assembly and served in the government of Sheikh Muji-
bur Rahman (q.v.) as a cabinet minister (1972-73). After the
assassination of Sheikh Mujibur Rahman, he split with the main
body of the Awami League and headed his own faction of the
Awami League. He joined President Ershad's party, the Jatiyo
Dal (q.v.), in 1983 and was named prime minister in 1986. He
was replaced by Moudud Ahmed (q.v.) in March 1988.

CHRISTIANITY. The Christian community was enumerated in the
1981 census as 275,000, with the largest concentrations in Mymensingh (45,000), Dhaka (44,000) and Khulna (35,000) regions.
The Christians in Mymensingh are principally members of tribal

groups, such as the Garos, whose main center of population is in the Indian state of Meghalaya to the north of Mymensingh. This group tends to be Protestant, most often Presbyterian. In the metropolitan areas of Dhaka, the Christians belong generally to two groups: Bengali converts and Eurasians (often described as "Anglo-Indians"). In each group Roman Catholicism predominates. Missionaries began to arrive in the 17th century and in British territory in the 19th century. The missions played and continue to play an important role in education and medical services. There is freedom to propagate religion, but donations from abroad to missions and missionaries are regulated by the government.

CLIMATE.   Located on the Tropic of Cancer, Bangladesh has a semi-tropical climate.   The seasons are a hot summer period from March to June; a warm, very humid monsoon period from June to September; a brief, dry, hot period from the end of the monsoon to mid-November; and a cooler, dry winter period from November to February.   Using Dhaka these seasons can be illustrated by the following monthly data:

Month	Mean Temperature (Fahrenheit)	Rainfall (Inches)	Humidity (Percent)
January	65	0.5	69
February	70	0.8	63
March	79	2.7	61
April	84	4.7	70
May	84	10.1	79
June	83	15.5	86
July	83	15.1	86
August	83	12.7	86
September	83	10.5	85
October	81	6.2	81
November	74	1.0	75
December	67	0.3	71

There is a wide variation in rainfall, ranging in 1984 from 188 inches at a station in Sylhet region in the northeast to 60 inches at Ishurdi in the northwest.   The weather system often includes violent storms, especially the cyclones which arise in the Bay of Bengal.   One in 1970 is believed to have claimed as many as half a million lives and resulted in the postponement of the scheduled general election from October to December of that year and in the affected areas along the coast until January 1971. Damage occurs from the high winds and from the influx of water. For example, as far inland as Khulna the water rose by two feet in the 1970 cyclone.   Independent Bangladesh has tried to meet the danger in two ways: the building of more solidly constructed homes, and the use of polders as in the Netherlands.

In 1988 the region suffered the worst flood in its history, when more than 25,000,000 people were made homeless.

CLIVE, ROBERT (Baron Clive of Plassey, 1725-1774). The victor
for the British at the Battle of Plassey (1757) and governor of
Bengal (1765-1767). He had earlier earned a reputation as an
administrator and a military leader in Madras. Subjected to a
parliamentary inquiry on his return to England, Clive eventually
committed suicide.

COMBINED OPPOSITION PARTIES (COP). A term which has several
meanings, but the one used most often is for the group that op-
posed Ayub Khan in the 1960s. The group included the Council
Muslim League (q.v.), the Jama' at-i-Islam (q.v.), the Nizam-i-
Islam Party (q.v.), the Pakistan Democratic Party, and other
smaller groups. The initial leader of the group was Khwaja
Nazimuddin (q.v.). The COP supported the candidature of Fatima
Jinnah, sister of Muhammad Ali Jinnah (q.v.), in the 1965 elec-
tion for the presidency. She lost to Ayub Khan (q.v.). The
COP by 1968 had ceased to function and was superseded by the
Pakistan Democratic Movement (q.v.).

COMILLA ACADEMY. The name of the East Pakistan unit of the
Pakistan Academy of Rural Development which was set up in the
early 1960s. The purpose was to apply social science theories to
practical problems of administration and to promote rural development. The project was aided by the Michigan State University.
The Comilla thana was used as a living laboratory to test projects
which could then be applied to other parts of the country. The
four major project areas were an improved model for rural administration, a model for reconstruction and expansion of rural
infrastructure, a model for utilization of surface and ground water
for irrigation and a new two tier cooperative system. Comilla is
usually used as a model for rural development in the international
development community. Akhtar Hameed Khan is credited for
the success of the program. Most of the research was undertaken
in the Matlab thana of Comilla district. One of the projects
that resulted was the Cholera Research Laboratory which was
funded by S.E.A.T.O.

COMMUNIST PARTY OF BANGLADESH. An outgrowth of the Communist Party of Pakistan which itself is an outgrowth of the Communist Party of India. The Communist Party of Pakistan was established in 1948 but was banned in 1954. The party existed as
an underground party till December 31, 1971, when it was given
legal recognition by the new government of Bangladesh. Lead by
Moni Singh (q.v.) the party is pro-Moscow in its orientation and
calls for political and economic reforms in social institutions which
can lead to the establishment of socialism. It cooperated with the
Awami League and was banned by Ziaur Rahman (q.v.) during
the early part of his regime. The Communist Party of Bangladesh was allowed to resume its legal existence in November 1978.

CONSTITUTION OF BANGLADESH, 1972. The Bangladesh constitution adopted a parliamentary system of government with a ceremonial president and a governing prime minister and cabinet. It was modeled very much on the constitution of India (1950), but without the federal concepts which were obviously not needed in the unitary Bangladeshi system. The constitution also enshrined the four pillars of Mujibbad (q.v.): nationalism, secularism, democracy and socialism. The constitution was modified first in January 1975, when an amendment was passed transforming the system to a presidential one with Mujibur Rahman (q.v.) as president. It was changed again in June 1975, when provisions were made for a one-party state. Military rulers including Ziaur Rahman (q.v.) and H. M. Ershad (q.v.) have also made changes so that the Bangladeshi political system is one in which the president is the focus of power to whom the cabinet and the parliament are subordinate.

CONSTITUTION OF PAKISTAN, 1956. Pakistan's first constitution was effective on March 23, 1956. Its adoption followed more than eight years of debate. It provided for a parliamentary system of government with a single house at the center and single chamber provincial assemblies in East and West Pakistan. The system was said to be federal but the bulk of the powers were given to the central government. A point of particular concern to the East Pakistanis was that of parity (q.v.). The constitution of 1956 was abrogated by the martial law decree of October 7, 1958. Elections were never held under this constitution.

CONSTITUTION OF PAKISTAN, 1962. The 1962 constitution of Pakistan was the second for the country. It was not passed by a constituent assembly but rather was promulgated by President Ayub Khan (q.v.) as his own "gift" to the nation. It provided for a strong presidential system with an indirectly elected national assembly. The president and the members of the national and provincial assemblies were to be elected by basic democrats (see Basic Democracy). Governors of the two provinces were appointed by the president and served according to his pleasure. The cabinet was also appointed by the president and was not responsible to the assembly. The parity (q.v.) system was continued so that East Pakistani votes counted for less than West Pakistani votes.

CONVENTION MUSLIM LEAGUE see PAKISTAN MUSLIM LEAGUE (CONVENTION)

CORNWALLIS, CHARLES CORNWALLIS, 1st MARQUESS (1738-1805). For Americans he is remembered as the commander of the British force that surrendered to Washington at Yorktown in 1781. His reputation in Britain was not tarnished and he served twice as governor general of India, 1786-1793, and again in 1805. During his first term, he introduced major reforms in the civil service of the East India Company that separated the governing role of the service from the private commercial activities of the company's officers. He also instituted the "permanent settlement" (q.v.) system for the lands in the Bengal presidency.

COUNCIL MUSLIM LEAGUE (CML). The name applied to a Muslim League group opposed to Ayub's Pakistan Muslim League (Convention) (q.v.). When parties were formed after the 1962 election, a group made up of members of the Muslim League (before parties were banned by Ayub in 1958) called a meeting of the council of the League (hence, the name of the new party). They revived the League through the revived council. Conversely, Ayub called a convention of Muslim Leaguers, bypassing the old council, to form his party. The CML became part of the Combined Opposition Parties (COP) (q.v.). Its first leader was Khwaja Nazimuddin (q.v.). After his death, the principal figure was Mian Mumtaz Muhammad Khan Daultana of the Punjab. It contested the 1970 election and won nine national assembly seats in West Pakistan but none in East Pakistan. It does not exist as such in either Pakistan or Bangladesh today.

CURZON OF KEDDLESTON, GEORGE NATHANIEL CURZON, 1st MARQUESS (1859-1925). A British statesman, viceroy and governor general of India, 1898-1905. Among his goals in India was the improvement, as he saw it, of the administrative system. One act taken in this direction in 1905 was the partitioning of the province (or presidency) of Bengal (see Bengal, Partition of [1905]). Curzon left India as the loser in a battle with Lord Kitchener, the then commander-in-chief of the Indian army. Curzon also made a major contribution to the preservation of Indian antiquities. His major post after leaving India was as British foreign secretary, 1919-1924.

- D -

DAS-HAQ PACT. An agreement in the early 1920s between the principal Muslim political figure in Bengal, Fazlul Haq (q.v.), and the leader of the Swarajist faction of the Indian National Congress, Chittaranjan Das (1870-1925). They agreed to limited cooperation to permit the system of dyarchy to work in the province and also to informal quotas to permit increased Muslim employment in government posts.

DELHI SULTANATE. The name applied to the Muslim kingdoms based in Delhi from 1206, when Turkish rulers first established a permanent base in India, to 1526 when the last dynasty was defeated in the battle of Panipat by the founder of the Mughal empire, Babar. There were five dynasties: Slave (or Mamluk), (1206-1290), Khalji (1290-1320), Tughluq (1320-1413), Sayyid (1414-1451), and Lodi (1451-1526). Before the setting up of the capital at Delhi, the Sena kingdom in Bengal fell to a general of the

Afghan sultanate based at Ghor. Bengal remained under at least the nominal control of Delhi until 1336, when Fakhruddin Mubarak Shah (q.v.) rebelled against the Tughluq dynasty. In 1346, Bengal became independent and remained so for almost two centuries under the Iliyas Shahi (q.v.) and Sayyid (q.v.) (not identical to the Delhi dynasty of the same name) dynasties. In 1538, forces of the Mughal emperor Humayun conquered Bengal which became dependent on Delhi once again, but as part of the successor empire to the Delhi sultanate.

DEMOCRATIC ACTION COMMITTEE. Formed in January 1969, was principally composed of the Awami League (q.v.), the National Awami Party (q.v.) of Wali Khan, and the Jama'at-i-Islam (q.v.). The action committee was set up to oppose the rule of President Ayub Khan (q.v.). Its purpose was the full and complete restoration of democracy in Pakistan. It issued an eight-point manifesto which included, among other points, the establishment of a federal parliamentary system of government, direct election by adult franchise and the release of popular leaders like Sheikh Mujibur Rahman (q.v.) and Z. A. Bhutto (q.v.).

DEMOCRATIC LEAGUE. Organized by defectors from the Awami League in August 1976. This party was established after the enactment of the Political Parties Regulation Act by President Ziaur Rahman (q.v.). The party was headed by Khondakar Mustaque Ahmed (q.v.) with the support of Mainul Hussain, who was the proprietor and managing editor of the Ittefaq newspaper (see Tofazzul Hussain). In mid-1977 the Democratic League split into two factions. Democratic League experienced a resurgence in 1980 after the release from jail of its leader, Mustaque Ahmed. In 1983 the Democratic League organized a national united front composed of right wing opposition parties.

DEMOCRATIC PARTY. Formed in December 1980 by the members of National Awami Party (q.v.) led by Maulana Bhashani (q.v.), was a dissident faction of the United People's Party, and two other participants in the 1979 Democratic Front: the Jatiya Gana Makti Union and the Gono Front. The Democratic Party was organized by Mirza Nurul Huda. He subsequently joined the Bangladesh Nationalist Party (q.v.).

DHAKA JAIL KILLINGS. Resulted in the death of Tajuddin Ahmad (q.v.), Syed Nazrul Islam (q.v.), Mansur Ali (q.v.) and A. H. M. Kamaruzzaman (q.v.) on November 3, 1977. Tajuddin Ahmad had been jailed during Mujibur Rahman's (q.v.) regime; the others following the August Coup (q.v.). Responsibility for the orders permitting the murders has not been fixed, although popular belief often assigns it to the majors (q.v.).

DHAKA, NAWAB OF (FAMILY). The family of the Nawab of Dhaka has produced a number of important political leaders in the region now comprising Bangladesh. The title is hereditary, but as a zamindar (landlord), not as a ruling prince. Among the members of the family have been Nawab Salimullah (q.v.), a founder of the Muslim League (q.v.); Khwaja Sir Nazimuddin (q.v.), whose last official position was prime minister of Pakistan; and Khwaja Shahabuddin (q.v.), Nazimuddin's younger brother, who served in several Pakistan cabinets. The last nawab in the Pakistan period was Hasan Askari (q.v.). The family was part of the National Elite (see Vernacular Elite) and has not been active in politics in independent Bangladesh although many collaterals are active in the administration. For example, General Khwaja Wasiuddin, son of Khwaja Shahabuddin and a former Pakistan army officer, has been a Bangladeshi ambassador. On the other hand, another collateral, Khwaja Khairuddin, is the leader of a splinter of the Muslim League in Pakistan.

DIRECT ACTION DAY. August 16, 1946, was a day set aside by the Muslim League for work stoppages (hartals) and demonstrations to emphasize the League's demand for the partition of India. The day had been agreed on at a meeting of Muslim League legislators in New Delhi on July 27, following the Congress rejection of the Cabinet Mission Plan (q.v.). The meeting also endorsed a single state of Pakistan as opposed to the plural "states" used in the Lahore Resolution (q.v.). The day was peaceful except in Calcutta where serious violence between Muslims and Hindus occurred. Suhrawardy (q.v.) was prime minister of Bengal at the time.

DIWANI OF BENGAL. Granted to the British East India Company by the Mughul emperor Shah Alam II in 1765. It gave the right to the company to collect taxes in the province of Bengal with portions going to the emperor and the nawab of Murshidabad (successors to Mir Jafar [q.v.]) and the remainder being used by the British.

DUDU MIA (1819-1862). His real name was Muhammad Moshini and he was the son of Haji Shariatullah (q.v.). He furthered the organizational setup of the Faraizi (q.v.) movement by dividing East Bengal into a number of regions and appointing persons to head each of the regions. He was able to keep himself well informed about all forms of suppression and take countermeasures against them. He propagated the idea that land belongs to Allah and that no one has permanent rights over land. He worked extensively for equality and welfare of the poor. For his activities he was arrested a number of times and tried but was never convicted of any crime. In 1857 he was imprisoned and died in 1862.

DUTTA, MICHAEL MODHUSHADAN (1824-1873). Poet and playwright, the first Bengali poet to use the sonnet technique in his poems. In 1840 he converted to Christianity. In 1849 two significant works--Captive Lady and Vision of Past--were published. He obtained a Bar-at-Law degree from England in 1866 and joined the

Calcutta bar. For a while he served as an editor of the Hindu Patriot.

DYARCHY. The term used to describe the system of provincial government created by the Government of India Act of 1919 (q.v.) (the Montagu-Chelmsford Act). Elected members became a majority in the legislative councils of the provinces and they would control, as in a parliamentary system, the ministers heading the "nation-building departments." These departments included education, agriculture, public works and health. The other departments, which represented the "steel frame" of British rule including home, finance and revenue would remain under the control of the governor through executive councilors appointed by and responsible to him. In operation, however, many of the executive councilor posts came to be held by Indians, most of whom had previous experience as ministers. Dyarchy was abolished at the provincial level by the Government of India Act of 1935 (q.v.) which created a system of provincial autonomy.

- E -

EAST BENGAL. The official name of the territory which is now Bangladesh from independence in 1947 to the enactment of legislation which consolidated the provinces in the west wing to a single province ("one-unit") in 1955, as part of the process of adopting the Constitution of 1956 of Pakistan (q.v.). The Indian portion of the pre-1947 province of Bengal was (and is) designated West Bengal with its capital at Calcutta.

EAST PAKISTAN. The official name for the territory which now comprises Bangladesh from 1955 until Bangladeshi independence in 1971. The territory was often also referred to informally as the "east wing."

EDUCATION. The literacy rate in Bangladesh was reported as 23.8 percent of the population aged five or older. Female literacy is lower than male; data for 1981 show male literacy as 31.0 percent and female as 16.0 percent. Education is not compulsory but is free at the primary level beginning at age five and continuing for five years. In 1983-84, there were 43,865 primary schools, reportedly enrolling 72.9 percent of the children aged five to nine. This figure is probably inflated, as it appears to include children who attended for any portion of the school year rather than those who attended the entire school year. At the secondary level, perhaps a more accurate figure, attendance of those aged ten to fourteen was reported to be 22.17 percent.

There are six universities in Bangladesh: comprehensive universities at Dhaka, Chittagong, Rajshahi and Jehangirnagar (a suburb of Dhaka); an engineering university in Dhaka; and an agricultural university at Mymensingh. It is reported that 2.0

percent of those between the ages of 15 and 24 attended universities in 1983-84. Of these students, 83.8 percent were male and 16.2 percent female. Data indicate that females tend to study in the arts faculties; of the students in the Faculty of Arts at Dhaka University, 65.8 percent were male and 34.2 percent female. Education does not receive a large share of the budget. Per capita allocations for all levels of education in 1983-84 were Taka 50 (less than $2). Much of the pre-university education takes place in privately operated schools rather than state schools. These private institutions vary widely in quality from the very good schools often run by Christian mission groups to those at the other end of the scale often operated by entrepreneurs for profit. The vocational education system can best be described as very weak. There are also a substantial number of Islamic primary schools (madrasahs) of varying quality that are attached to mosques and other religious endowments.

EIGHTEEN-POINTS. A program which was announced by President Ershad (q.v.) in March 1983 for the economic and political revival of Bangladesh. Economic self-sufficiency, democratization of the political system and decentralization of the administrative system provided the major thrust of the program.

ELECTIVE BODIES (DISQUALIFICATION) ORDER (EBDO). Issued in April 1959. The purpose was to inquire into allegations of misconduct by any person who held any public office or position including membership of any elective body in the country. Persons appearing before EBDO tribunal were not allowed assistance of counsel. Proceedings were held under Code of Civil Procedure and not Code of Criminal Procedure. A number of officials were disqualified under the order from participating or holding public office for seven years. The order was repealed in December 1960, but the disqualification of those already disqualified continued until the end of 1967.

ERSHAD, HUSSAIN MUHAMMAD (b. 1930). A regular army officer, rising to the rank of lieutenant colonel in the Pakistan army. During the civil war of 1971, he was posted in Pakistan and detained there, returning to Bangladesh in 1973. He reached the rank of major general in 1975 and was appointed deputy chief of staff. He succeeded Ziaur Rahman (q.v.) as chief of staff in 1978, when the latter resigned from the army, and was promoted to lieutenant general in 1979. He led a coup against the elected government of Abdus Sattar (q.v.) in March 1982, and became chief martial law administrator. He assumed the presidency in December 1984. He was elected president for a five-year term in October 1986; he ran as a civilian, having resigned from the army, as the candidate of the Jatiyo Dal (q.v.) of which he was the chairman. His title as chief martial law administrator was abolished in November 1986, with the ending of martial law.

- F -

FAKHRUDDIN MUBARAK SHAH (d. 1346). Led a rebellion against
the Tughluq dynasty of the Delhi sultanate in 1336. On the
death of the then governor in 1336, Fakhruddin proclaimed himself the independent ruler of Sonargaon (q.v.). In 1346, he was
superseded by the Iliyas Shahi dynasty (q.v.).

FARAIZI MOVEMENT (or Faraidiyyah). A Bengali Muslim movement
which had its antecedents in the Wahhabi movement in Arabia.
It was founded by Shariatullah (q.v.) in the first half of the
19th century. It preached the oneness of Allah and opposed any
deviations from a strict interpretation of the Quran and Sunnah.
Shariatullah was followed by his son, Dudu Mia (1819-1862) (q.v.),
whose actions in opposition to Hindu landlords and British officials ended in his arrest in 1847. The movement soon weakened
although followers remain. The Kabir family (q.v.) is descended
from the leaders.

FARID AHMAD (1923-1971). Resigned from the government service
because of his support for the language movement of 1952. He
was the leader of the Nizam-i-Islam (q.v.) political party. He
served as a member of the Pakistan Constituent Assembly in 1955
and was a member of the National Assembly in 1962. In 1964 he
joined the Combined Opposition Parties (q.v.) and was elected
as a representative of the party to the National Assembly. He
joined the opposition in its movement to oust President Ayub Khan
(q.v.) in 1969. He was opposed to the war of liberation and
collaborated with the Pakistani armed forces. He was an adviser
to the Razzakar Bahini (q.v.) and a leading member of the Peace
Committees (q.v.) which were set up to coerce Bengalis to continue the idea of a united Pakistan.

FARRAKA BARRAGE. At the core of the Ganges waters dispute between Bangladesh and India. The idea of a barrage near Farraka was first mooted in the early 20th century. The barrage
would divert water from the Ganges River through canals and
the Bhagirati and Hooghly rivers to reduce salinity in the Hooghly
at Calcutta and to augment its flow. This would assure Calcutta
of a greater supply of drinking water and would lessen the silt-
ing of Calcutta harbor. After independence, India revived the
idea and built the barrage. Bangladesh claims that it needs the
water withdrawn to reduce salinity and improve irrigation in
Khulna division.
    India has proposed that a link canal be built transferring
water from the Brahmaputra River to the Ganges above Farraka
so that adequate flow would be available both for Calcutta and
Khulna division. Bangladesh has countered with a plan that
would entail additional storage dams in Nepal to regulate better
the flow of the Ganges during the low flow season (April-June);
during other times the flow is usually sufficient for both India

and Bangladesh. The two countries have reached an interim agreement on sharing the water during the low-flow period, but a final agreement has not been made.

FAZLUL HAQ, (MOULVI) ABUL KASEM (1873-1962). The leading Bengali Muslim political figure in the pre-independence period and for many years after independence. He was a member of the Bengal Legislative Council, 1913-1920, constituted under the Government of India Act of 1909 (q.v.) and again, 1921-1935, under the Dyarchy (q.v.) system established by the Government of India Act of 1919 (q.v.). He was a member of the Muslim League (q.v.), 1913-1942, until his membership was ended in a dispute with Muhammad Ali Jinnah (q.v.). After the elections following the passage of the Government of India Act of 1935 (q.v.), Fazlul Haq served as prime minister of Bengal, 1937-1943. He was the founder (in 1927) of the Krishak Praja Party (q.v.), leading it in the 1937 and 1946 elections. In the latter, the party was badly defeated by the Muslim League although Fazlul Haq retained his own seat. The party was then dissolved.

After independence, he was advocate general of East Bengal, 1947-1954, but resigned to revive his party under the altered name Krishak Sramik Party (q.v.) and to enter the United Front (q.v.) with the Awami League (q.v.). The front swept to victory and Fazlul Haq became chief minister briefly in 1954, but his government was dismissed by the central government of Pakistan. With a partial settlement with the central government, he became a central minister, 1955-1956, and governor of East Pakistan, 1956-1958. He retired from politics after the coup of Ayub Khan (q.v.) in 1958.

FAZLUR RAHMAN (1905-1966). A lawyer from Dhaka, was a prominent Muslim League (q.v.) political figure both before and after independence. He was elected in 1937 and 1946 to the Bengal Legislative Assembly and became a minister in 1946. He was a member of the cabinet of Pakistan, 1947-1953, but was removed by the then governor general, Ghulam Muhammad, largely as a result of his advocacy of Bengali positions on such issues as language and economic parity, despite his remaining in the Muslim League. He was reelected to the constituent assembly in 1955. After martial law was proclaimed by Ayub Khan (q.v.) in 1958, Fazlur Rahman continued to be associated with the Muslim League (the Council Muslim League [q.v.] in his case after 1962) until his death in an automobile accident.

FOREIGN POLICY. Bangladesh is a member of the Non-Aligned Movement and of the Group of 77. It is also an active member of the Organization of the Islamic Conference (q.v.). Bangladesh is a member of the (British) Commonwealth of Nations. It became a member of the United Nations (q.v.) in 1974 and was elected to the Security Council in 1978. In 1985, its foreign minister, Humayun Rashid Chowdhury, was elected president of the General

Assembly. For relations with specific countries see separate entries for Afghanistan, Burma, China, India, Middle East, Pakistan, Union of Soviet Socialist Republics and the United States. See also Islamic Conference.

- G -

GANOTANTRIK DAL. A short-lived political party led by Mahmud Ali (q.v.). It was leftist and attempted to be non-communal. It gained its only (and very small) electoral success when it was part of the United Front (q.v.) in 1954.

GAUR (also known as Lakhnauti). Now in ruins, located in Malda district, West Bengal. It is believed to have been founded by a Sena king and used as his capital. It and its neighboring sites of Pandua and Tanda served as capitals during various periods of Muslim control of Bengal from the beginning of the 13th century to the latter part of the 16th century. Several ruins are of historical and tourist interest.

GHAZNAVI, SIR ABDUL HALIM (1879-1956). A politician and social activist, was a zamindar who received all his education outside India. He actively participated in political, economic and educational movements in India. In 1929 he was the President of the All-India Muslim Conference, a short-lived rival of the Muslim League (q.v.). He participated in the Round Table Conference in London. He served both as chairman of the Calcutta Chamber of Commerce and the sheriff of Calcutta. He was a brother of Sir Abdul Karim Ghazavni (q.v.).

GHAZNAVI, SIR ABDUL KARIM (1872-1971). Educated outside India, was a politician and social activist. He was a member of the Imperial Legislative Council, 1909-1916, and member of the Governor-General's Council, 1913-1916, representing the Muslims of Bengal. As a representative of the British raj he went to Syria, Palestine, Egypt and Saudi Arabia. He was the author of Muslim Education in Bengal. He was a brother of Sir Abdul Halim Ghaznavi (q.v.).

GHULAM MUHAMMAD (1895-1956). Governor general of Pakistan, 1951-1955. Although he was born in Lahore, his family home was in East Punjab (now part of India). Before independence he was a civil servant and later in business. He was finance minister of Pakistan prior to succeeding Khwaja Nazimuddin (q.v.) as governor general.

GOVERNMENT OF INDIA ACT OF 1909. Also known as the Morley-Minto Act after, respectively, Lord Morley, Secretary of State for India in the British cabinet, and Lord Minto (q.v.), viceroy of India. The act was a major step along the route toward Indian self-government. The act admitted Indians to the executive

councils (i.e., cabinets) of the governor general and the lieutenant governors of the provinces. It provided for election of
Indians to the legislative councils at the central and provincial
levels, although a majority of the members (including some Indians) were appointed. The act also introduced the system of
separate electorates (q.v.) for Muslims and "others" (i.e., primarily Hindus, but not all in this category were Hindu by any
means).

GOVERNMENT OF INDIA ACT OF 1919. Also known as the Montagu-
Chelmsford Act after, respectively, Edwin Montagu, Secretary
of State for India in the British cabinet, and Lord Chelmsford,
the viceroy. At the central level the act created two legislative
houses, the (upper) Council of State and the (lower) Central
Legislative Assembly. In each house, elected Indians would form
a majority. However, the final powers continued to be held by
the viceroy and no concept of parliamentary responsibility was introduced. The viceroy's executive council of seven would have
three Indian members. At the provincial level, the legislative
councils would also have a majority of elected Indians. A limited
admission of the principle of responsibility was the system of
dyarchy (q.v.).

GOVERNMENT OF INDIA ACT OF 1935. The last such act passed by
the British parliament before independence. At the provincial
level, the act provided for autonomy in the sense that responsible governments were introduced in each of the provinces. The
prime minister (as he was then designated, the title would become "chief minister" after independence in both India and Pakistan) and his cabinet must enjoy the confidence of the legislative
assembly. "Legislative assembly," as a term, replaced "legislative council," although in a few provinces, including Bengal,
there was also an upper chamber which retained the name
"legislative council."

In the provinces, in the case of a breakdown of the cabinet
government or in a financial emergency (e.g., failure to pass a
budget) the governor retained powers to act to permit government to continue. At the center, a federal system was contemplated that would include the princely states. The princes did
not agree to this arrangement so the system of dyarchy (q.v.),
which was to have been introduced at the center, was never
adopted. Power, therefore, was distributed as under the Government of India Act of 1919 (q.v.). The 1935 act, as amended by
the India Independence Act of 1947, served as the "constitution"
of both India and Pakistan until each adopted its own constitution.

GRAM SARKAR. A village government scheme introduced by President Ziaur Rahman (q.v.) in 1980. Each Gram Sarkar was to be
responsible for a number of activities including family problems,
population control, food production, and law and order. A twelve-
member committee was to head the unit with two members coming

from each of the following groups: landless peasants, women, landed peasants, shopkeepers, fisherman/artisans. The chairman and the secretary were to be chosen by these ten members.

- H -

HABIBULLAH, ABU MUHAMMAD (1911-1984). A well-known historian and educationist who was the president of the Asiatic Society of Bengal, Bangladesh History Association and served two terms as the curator of the Dhaka Museum. He wrote a number of books, including the Foundation of Muslim Rule in India (1975). For his research in Bengali literature he was awarded the Bangla Academy award in 1980.

HAMOODUR RAHMAN COMMISSION. Appointed by Pakistani president Bhutto in 1972 to look into the political and military causes of the loss of East Pakistan. The head of the commission, himself a Bengali, was a retired chief justice of the Supreme Court. The report has not been released to the public. This has caused speculation that the report was critical of Bhutto as well as the military and other political figures.

HASAN ASKARI, NAWAB KHWAJA (1921-1984). The Last Nawab of Dhaka during the Pakistan period. He assisted the Pakistan army during the war of liberation and stayed in Pakistan. A military officer by profession he joined the Indian armed forces as a commissioned officer and served in the Burma front during World War II. From 1948-1961 he was in the Pakistan Army. In 1962 he retired from service and became a member of the Pakistan National Assembly and later communication minister of East Pakistan.

HASINA WAJID see SHEIKH HASINA WAJID

HASTINGS, WARREN (1732-1818). Came to India in 1750 as a clerk in the East India Company and rose to become the first governor general of India in 1773. He had been named the governor of Bengal in 1772. He abolished the diwani (q.v.) set up by Clive (q.v.) and began to collect revenue directly. Payments to the Mughal emperor were also discontinued. He left India in 1780. He was accused by his opponents of financial improprieties, but his impeachment by the British parliament ended in acquittal on all counts.

HEALTH DELIVERY. The health delivery system of Bangladesh can best be classified as weak. The ratio (1981) of population to doctors is 9,700 to 1, and to nurses 19,400 to 1. While these data refer to the country as a whole, there is a strong bias toward urban areas and the rural areas have much lower medical coverage. Infant mortality was 123 per 10,000 in 1985. The child death rate (aged 1-4) was 18 per 10,000. Life expectancy at birth was 51 (1981), with male expectancy at 50 and female at 51. In 1985, the daily caloric supply per person was 1,899, a decline from 1,964 calories in 1965. The country is subject to a number of the debilitating diseases often associated with tropical areas and with areas in which the availability of safe drinking water and the provision of adequate sewage facilities is rare. Most prevalent are diarrheal diseases, including cholera, that are among the principal causes of the high infant mortality rate. The government is placing a high priority on health delivery and is utilizing foreign assistance as well as its own resources to improve conditions.

HINDUISM. Hinduism was presumably the religion of all Bengalis prior to the expansion of Buddhism during the Pala dynasty (q.v.). With the Sena dynasty (q.v.), Brahmanical Hinduism revived briefly before the advent of Islam in the 13th century. According to the 1981 census, there were about 10.5 million Hindus in Bangladesh, comprising 12.1 percent of the population. This showed a considerable decrease from the last pre-independence census, that of 1961, when the Hindu population was recorded as 18.4 percent of the population. The substantial out-migration to India during the 1971 civil war was not offset, by any means, by the return of the Hindu refugees. The regions (former districts) with the highest ratio of Hindus are Khulna (27.2 percent), Dinajpur (21.9 percent), Jessore (19.6 percent), Faridpur (18.8 percent), and Sylhet (18.0 percent).

Although census data are not reported for 1981, it is widely believed that the majority of the Hindus in Bangladesh belong to the Scheduled Castes (the group once described as "untouchables," or in Gandhi's term, Harijans, i.e., children of God). In the 1961 census, caste (q.v.) Hindus were enumerated separately and represented 53.2 percent of all Hindus. As a basis for comparison, the 1961 census of India indicated that 12.6 percent of Indian Hindus were from the Scheduled Castes. It is clear that the two major out-migrations of Hindus, in the early 1950s and in 1971, were comprised primarily of caste Hindus. In the 1954 election, Hindus voted separately from Muslims under the system of separate electorates (q.v.). In elections since then, the system of joint electorates (see Separate Electorates) has been used. Hindus are under no legal restrictions and several have served in parliament and in the cabinet. Data appear to show that Hindu voters have favored the Awami League (q.v.).

HOSSAIN, KAMAL (b. 1937). A British-educated barrister who was a close associate of Sheikh Mujibur Rahman (q.v.). He was elected to the National Assembly in a by-election in 1971. After independence he served in the Mujib cabinets as minister of law and then as minister of foreign affairs. In the former post, he piloted the constitution bill. After Mujib's assassination, he went into self-imposed exile in England, but returned to run for the presidency in 1981 as the candidate of the Awami League (q.v.), being defeated by Abdus Sattar (q.v.). He has continued his association with the Awami League.

HUDA, MIRZA NURUL (b. 1919). An economist, civil servant and educator, was also finance minister of East Pakistan, 1965-1969, and, very briefly, governor, 1969. He was a member of the Pakistan Muslim League (q.v.) delegation to the roundtable conference held by Ayub Khan (q.v.) in 1969, in opposition to the Democratic Action Committee (q.v.). He returned to teaching during the Mujibur Rahman (q.v.) regime, but joined the cabinet of Ziaur Rahman (q.v.) in 1975 as minister of commerce and later as minister of finance and planning until 1980 (he also held temporary charge of other ministries during this period). Nurul Huda was the appointed vice-president during all but the last few days of the presidency of Abdus Sattar (q.v.).

HUQ, MUHAMMAD SHAMSUL (b. 1910). A noted educationist who was vice chancellor of Rajshahi University (1965-1969), served also in the Pakistan cabinet of Yahya Khan (q.v.) (1969-1971) and in the Bangladesh cabinets of Ziaur Rahman (q.v.) (1977-1981) and Abdus Sattar (q.v.) (1981-1982). In the Bangladeshi cabinets he was minister of foreign affairs. He was instrumental in bringing to fruition the goal of Zia to form the South Asian Association for Regional Cooperation (SAARC) (q.v.). It is reported that he was offered the presidency by H. M. Ershad (q.v.) in 1982, but refused in opposition to the military coup which ousted the elected civilian government of Sattar. After leaving office, he has headed the Bangladesh Institute of International and Strategic Studies, an important and influential "think tank."

HYE, MUHAMMAD ABDUL (1919-1969). An educationist and philanthropist, was the chairman of the Bengali department of Dhaka University when the central government of Pakistan proposed a Roman script for Bengali. He was instrumental in organizing opposition to such a move by the government. He was well known for his research in Bengali language pronunciation and phonetics and for his effort he was recognized by the Bangla Academy in 1961.

- I -

IBRAHIM KHAN (1894-1978). An educationist, litterateur and a social activist, participated in the Non-Cooperation movement and the Khalafat movement in the early 1920s. He joined the Congress in 1920 and the Muslim League (q.v.) in 1937. He was a member of the Pakistan National Assembly in 1962. He established a number of schools and colleges of which the Korotia College in Tangail, which he established with the financial assistance of Wajid Ali Khan Panni (q.v.), is the best known.

IBRAHIM, MUHAMMAD (1894-1966). A member of the judicial service and a firm believer in parliamentary democracy, was appointed a justice of the Dhaka High Court in 1950, vice chancellor of Dhaka University in 1956 and the Central Law Minister in 1958 during the Ayub Khan (q.v.) government. It was during his leadership in the law ministry that the Muslim Family Law Ordinance was passed in 1962.

ILIYAS SHAHI DYNASTY. Ruled Bengal from 1346 to 1490. It was founded by Shamsuddin Iliyas Shah following a period of turmoil during the previous decade as local Bengali chiefs overthrew the rule of the governor of the Tughluq Dynasty of the Delhi sultanate. Iliyas Shah was able to repulse an attack by the Tughluqs during the 1350s and established his capital at Pandua, near Gaur (q.v.). The dynasty was overthrown in 1490 by the founder of the Sayyid Dynasty (q.v.), Alauddin Hussain Shah (q.v.).

INDIA. India contributed greatly to the independence of Bangladesh by providing refuge, sanctuary, supplies, training and arms to the Mukti Bahini (q.v.), the Bangladeshi personnel in rebellion against Pakistan. In late November 1971 (early December according to Indian sources), India intervened directly in the conflict and, with the Mukti Bahini, defeated the Pakistani forces. The latter surrendered at Dhaka on December 16, 1971, in a ceremony which excluded representatives of the Mukti Bahini and the Government of Bangladesh in exile. This began a series of events that cooled relations between the two countries. Others included the commissioning by India of Farraka Barrage (q.v.), the overstaying (by Bangladeshi standards) of Indian troops in the Chittagong Hill Tracts (q.v.), and the taking of Pakistani military equipment by India. Nonetheless, during the period of Sheikh Mujibur Rahman (q.v.) relations were close and culminated in the signing of a treaty of friendship between the two nations (see India-Bangladesh Treaty) in 1972.

India, under Indira Gandhi, took the assassination of Mujib in August 1975 as an event aimed against India. India supported insurgents under an opponent of Ziaur Rahman (q.v.). Although relations have improved under Morarji Desai and Rajiv Gandhi in India and H. M. Ershad (q.v.) in Bangladesh, a number of problems remain. Chief among these is the unresolved Farraka dispute. Others include the land (see Berubari Enclave) and maritime boundaries, trade relations in which Bangladesh has a sizable deficit, the migration of Bangladeshis into Assam and other northeastern states of India, and the possible interference of each country in the other's tribal problems. Both countries are members of the South Asian Association for Regional Cooperation (q.v.). The three principal Bangladeshi leaders (Mujib, Zia and Ershad) made official visits to India.

INDIA-BANGLADESH TREATY. A 25-year agreement between the

two countries contracted in March 1972. It is formally termed a treaty of friendship, cooperation and peace. It was signed as India completed its withdrawal from Bangladesh, and is seen by some as a quid pro quo for the removal of Indian troops from the Chittagong Hill Tracts (q.v.). The treaty, which in itself is not exceptional from the general class of treaties between neighbors, was seen by some Bangladeshis as substituting Indian dominance for that of Pakistan.

INDO-PAKISTAN WAR OF 1965. A conflict over Kashmir. Pakistani forces attacked Indian troops in Kashmir; India responded by attacking along the Punjab border and farther south. The war on the Punjab boundary began on September 6 and a cease-fire on all fronts came in three weeks. There was no conflict involving territory in East Pakistan. East Pakistanis, nonetheless, were concerned that the concentration of Pakistani troops in the west wing left them vulnerable to an Indian attack. This formed a basis for the last of the Six Points (q.v.) announced by Sheikh Mujibur Rahman (q.v.) in January 1966.

INDO-PAKISTAN WAR OF 1971. An outgrowth of the civil war in East Pakistan that began on March 26. India provided, early on, a sanctuary and training areas for the Mukti Bahini (q.v.) and a home for the Bangladesh government in exile. It also served as a home for a large number of refugees (some estimates are as high as ten million) and as a provider of arms for the Mukti Bahini. In late November, Indian forces began to operate with the Mukti Bahini against Pakistani troops. Indian troops captured Dhaka on December 16, ending the conflict in the east. There were also actions in December in the west between Pakistan and India, but a unilateral cease-fire declaration by India was accepted de facto by Pakistan on December 18.

INDUSTRY. Industry contributed but 14 percent of the gross domestic product (GDP) of Bangladesh (1985) and employed 6 percent of the labor force (1980). The employment is reported to have been 11 percent in 1985. Manufacturing produced 8 percent of the GDP in 1985. Overall industrial growth between 1980 and 1985 was at the annual rate of 4.7 percent; that of manufacturing, 2.0 percent. By sector the share in the manufacturing segment in 1984 was food and agricultural processing, 15 percent; textiles, 39 percent; machinery and transport equipment, 6 percent; chemicals and fertilizers, 24 percent; and "others," 16 percent. Of these categories textiles and, to a lesser extent, agricultural processing are important export areas. The relatively high figure for chemicals and fertilizers recognizes the importance of domestic natural gas resources.

A serious problem for Bangladesh is the decline in productivity: with 1980 as the base of 100, productivity was 89 in 1985 compared with 116 in 1960. Similarly, earnings by labor with the same base year were 78 in 1985 (the datum for 1960 is not available). One perhaps valid explanation of the decline in productivity and earnings is the rapid nationalization of industries in the regime of Mujibur Rahman (q.v.) and the resultant inefficiencies. The governments of Ziaur Rahman (q.v.) and H. M. Ershad (q.v.), especially the latter, have done much to denationalize industry and banking and in general to liberalize the economy. The damage done during the civil war also contributed to the decline in industry; industrial output did not exceed pre-independence levels until 1978-79. The effect of the liberalization is yet to be seen.

ISLAM. Islam is professed by 86.7 percent of the population of Bangladesh, according to the 1981 census. Almost all Bengali Muslims are Sunnis with a small number of Ithna Ashari Shia and of Ismaili Shia. Most of the latter two sects are descendants of non-Bengalis who migrated to Bengal during the period of Muslim rule from Delhi or later. With more than 75 million Muslims (1981), Bangladesh ranks after Indonesia and with India and Pakistan as a state with the highest number of Muslims. This has given Bangladesh an important position in the Islamic Conference Organization (q.v.).

Leadership among Muslims includes the local mulla or imam, the maulana who is presumed to be learned in Islam (a member of the ulema), and the pirs who preside over shrines usually dedicated to deceased sufi saints. There is among Sunnis no designated hierarchy. The Islamic leadership is generally confined to religious matters and political activity is limited; there is no significant fundamentalism in Bangladesh. Rather, Islam is generally considered to be a personal matter and there is no state enforcement of Islamic law or custom. Nonetheless, Islam in the personal sense is deeply rooted in the country.

Bengali Muslims, as all subcontinental Muslims, formally eschew caste (q.v.), but in practice, hereditary groupings are recognized and in rural Bangladesh are important in such rites as marriage. Within the Muslim society certain distinctions are admitted: the ashraf, the upper class and often members of the National Elite (q.v.); the ajlaf, a middle urban and rural class that has included many of the leaders of the Vernacular Elite (q.v.); and the arzal, the lower classes.

ISLAMIC CONFERENCE. The Islamic Conference was established in 1971. The secretariat of the Organization of the Islamic Conference (OIC) is located in Jiddah. The second summit of the OIC was held in Lahore, Pakistan, in February 1974. Bangladesh was not invited to the meeting. Through the efforts of several Muslim heads of state, Pakistani Prime Minister Zulfiqar Ali Bhutto (q.v.) was prevailed upon to invite Mujibur Rahman (q.v.) to attend. Pakistani recognition of Bangladesh as well as that of most Arab nations dates from this meeting although formal diplomatic relations were not established in most cases (including Pakistan) until after the death of Mujib. Bangladesh has been active

in the OIC and presented an unsuccessful candidate for the
secretary generalship in 1985. Dhaka served as the venue for
the 1983 meeting of the foreign ministers of the group.

ISLAMIC DEMOCRATIC LEAGUE. An ultra-conservative political party
composed of members of the Nizam-i-Islam (q.v.), the Jama'at-i-
Islam (q.v.) and two smaller parties, the People's Democratic
Party and the Islamic Ganotantrik Dal. It was established in
1976. Its leader, Maulana Abdur Rahim, contested the 1981
presidential election. The party is against westernization and
secularism and aims to make Bangladesh an Islamic republic.
One of its demands is that the national anthem of Bangladesh be
changed because it was written by Rabindranath Tagore (q.v.),
who was a Hindu.

ISMAIL, KHAN BAHADUR MUHAMMAD (1871–1945). Received the
title of Khan Bahadur by the British. He was a contemporary
of Sir Salimullah (q.v.). He organized the Krishak Praja Party
(q.v.) in Mymensingh district of Bangladesh. He was actively
involved with the Mymensingh district council serving as its
vice chairman from 1906 to 1920 and as chairman from 1920 to
1929. He was a lawyer by profession.

ISPAHANI FAMILY. A Shia Muslim business family which originated
in Iran, as the name indicates. They moved to India in the 18th
century. Based first in Madras, the family achieved prominence
in Bengal before 1947. After Pakistani independence, the group
maintained headquarters in Karachi and Dhaka. Activities included
tea and jute manufacture, insurance and banking. The group
also established Orient Airlines, the predecessor of the nationalized Pakistani International Airlines. In the 1960s, the group
was ranked 8th among Pakistani business houses in assets. Mirza
Abol Hasan Ispahani (q.v.) was a prominent political figure as
well as a part of the managing group of the family. The family,
since 1971, has maintained holdings in both Bangladesh and
Pakistan.

ISPAHANI, MIRZI ABOL HASAN (1901-1981). A member of the important business house of the Ispahani family (q.v.), was a close
associate and later biographer of Muhammad Ali Jinnah (q.v.).
He was a member of the Bengal legislature before independence
and the constituent assembly afterward. He was the first Pakistani ambassador to the United States (1947-1952) and later high
commissioner to the United Kingdom and a central minister. In
politics, he represented the small Muslim commercial and industrial
community in Bengal and would oppose the Awami League (q.v.)
and Husain Shahid Suhrawardy (q.v.) in their regionalist goals.

- J -

JAGODAL (acronym for Jatiyatabadi Ganotantrik Dal). A political party formed, largely by nonpolitical figures, to support President Ziaur Rahman (q.v.). In 1978, it merged into the broader Bangladesh Nationalist Party (BNP) (q.v.), although a small group remains, retaining the name JAGODAL.

JALALUDDIN AHMAD, MOLLAH (1926-1979). A close friend of Sheikh Mujibur Rahman (q.v.), was a lawyer by profession. A member of the Muslim League (q.v.) student organization during the movement for Pakistan, he was a very active participant and worked extensively during the Sylhet Referendum (q.v.). He left the Muslim League to join the Awami League (q.v.) in 1949. He was, for nearly 29 years, a member of the Working Committee of the Awami League. He actively supported the war of liberation and after the independence of Bangladesh held a number of ministerial positions. He was among the very few members of the Awami League who was elected to the National Assembly of Bangladesh in 1979.

JAMA'AT-I-ISLAM. A political party generally described as Islamic fundamentalist. It was founded in India in 1941 by Maulana Syed Abu Ala Maududi. It supports the return of the political system to that of the period of the first four caliphs (632-661). While Maududi's writings have had an impact throughout the Islamic world, the party has had but little success in Pakistani elections. Its principal base was in West Pakistan. In Bangladesh it is among the lesser political groups in electoral terms, but has some influence through the network of Islamic organizations. Many of its Bangladeshi members have associated with the Islamic Democratic League (q.v.).

JASIMUDDIN (1903-76). A Bangladeshi author of repute. He is principally known for his collection of traditional stories about village life, turing them into ballads depicting the joys and sorrows of the Bangladeshi countryside. By marriage he was related to Kazi Nazrul Islam (q.v.).

JATIYA SAMAJTANTRIK DAL (JSD). Established in October 1972. It was organized by Abdur Rab and Shajahan Siraj, who were student leaders at Dhaka University and also members of the Awami League (q.v.). Two distinguished members of the Bangladesh army, Colonel Abu Taher and Major M. A. Jalil, also provided leadership to the party. It opposed Awami League's Mujibbad (q.v.). It is a socialist and left-leaning political party intent on introducing scientific socialism in Bangladesh with comparatively young leaders. It came into prominence as a result of its influence in the army through such units as the Biplobi Shainik Sangsthan (Revolutionary Soldiers Organization) and Biplobi Gana Army (Revolutionary Peoples Army). Abu Taher (q.v.) assisted Ziaur Rahman (q.v.) in his rise to power. Ziaur Rahman later disassociated himself from Abu Taher and reduced the influence of JDG within the army. Abu Taher was later executed. After

1977, the party was banned but reemerged in 1978 favoring the parliamentary system. It is characterized as an anti-Indian, anti-Soviet and pro-Chinese political party. Like many other political parties of Bangladesh, it split into two factions in 1980. One splinter group is called Bangladesh Samajtantrik Dal (BSD) with the other retaining the original name.

JATIYO DAL. A political party formed to support President H. M. Ershad (q.v.). The party drew members primarily from the Bangladesh Nationalist Party (q.v.) which had been formed to support Ziaur Rahman (q.v.). It also drew some members from the Awami League (q.v.). It is a centrist party and favors denationalization of many industries that were nationalized during the period of Mujibur Rahman (q.v.). As is the case with most parties formed around an individual, it is weak in organization. The Jatiyo Dal won a slight majority in the parliamentary election of 1986. Its parliamentary leader, Mizanur Rahman Chowdhury (q.v.), became prime minister.

JATIYO RAKKHI BAHINI (also known as Rakkhi Bahini). Established by Sheikh Mujibur Rahman (q.v.) in mid-1972 as a village paramilitary security force. However, it soon came to be known as the personal security force and political enforcement body of the Awami League (q.v.). It functioned out of the presidential secretariat and reported directly to Sheikh Mujibur Rahman. Deemed by the Supreme Court of Bangladesh to be an organization which functioned without any rules of procedure or code of conduct, it was disbanded after the first military coup that took place in August 1975.

JINNAH, MUHAMMAD ALI (1876-1948). Known also as Qaid-i-Azam (great leader) by his admirers in Pakistan and in the Muslim League (q.v.), was the leader of the League in its struggle for the partition of India and the formation of a separate Pakistan. A London-trained barrister, he entered politics as a member of the Congress but joined the Muslim League as well in 1913. He was a key figure in the negotiation of an agreement between the Congress and the League in 1916 on the question of separate electorates (q.v.) for Muslims. Jinnah left the Congress in 1920 and, except for some time in the early thirties, continued to work for a special status for the Muslims whom he saw as a nation in India separate from the Hindus. With independence in 1947, he became general of Pakistan, a post he held until his death on September 11, 1948. Jinnah visited East Bengal only once as governor general (in March 1948) and, among other statements, he angered many East Bengalis by stating that Urdu would be the only official language of Pakistan.

- K -

KABIR FAMILY. Descended from Haji Shariatullah (q.v.), founder of the Faraizi Movement (q.v.). The generation active during the independence period has several members who were prominent in public life. Two elder brothers, Jehangir and Humayun (q.v.) remained in India; the former was a minister in the West Bengal government and the latter a minister in the Government of India under Jawaharlal Nehru. Two younger brothers, Alamgir and Akbar, were active in East Pakistan and Bangladesh; the former was a member of the police service and the latter was a minister in the government led by Ziaur Rahman (q.v.).

KABIR, HUMAYUN (1906-1969). A member of the Bengal Legislative Council, 1937-1947. He chose to remain in India where he became educational adviser to the government (1952-1956) and a minister in the central government (1957-1965). He wrote extensively on literature and history.

KAIKOBAD (1857-1951). Given the title of great poet for his work entitled Mohashoshan or great funeral pyre. His actual name was Muhammad Kazem Al-Quarashi. He received numerous awards and was the president of the Bengal Muslim Literature Society.

KAISER, KHAWAJA MUHAMMAD (1918-1985). A member of the Indian Police Service, joined the Pakistan Foreign Service in 1950. He served as Pakistani ambassador to Switzerland, Denmark and Norway and was high commissioner to Australia and New Zealand. As ambassador to China in 1971, he switched his allegiance from Pakistan to Bangladesh. From 1976 to 1982 he was the permanent representative of Bangladesh to the United Nations. He resigned from service in 1982 but was later called on by Bangladesh to be its ambassador to China. He was instrumental in improving the relationship between China and Bangladesh. Reportedly, he was offered the presidency of Bangladesh by General Ershad (q.v.) but refused.

KAMARUZZAMAN, A. H. M. (1926-1975). Assassinated in what is known as the Dhaka jail killings (q.v.), was president of the Awami League (q.v.) in 1974. A member of the first provisional government of Bangladesh, he also served as the Bangladesh commerce minister. He was elected to the National Assembly of Pakistan in 1962.

KHAFILUDDIN AHMAD (1899-1972). Joined the Muslim League in 1926 but resigned from the party in 1939 because of the domination of the Nawab of Dhaka family (q.v.). He was law minister in the 1954 United Front (q.v.) cabinet. In 1956 he joined the Awami League (q.v.) and was arrested by the martial law authorities in 1958. He reemerged in politics in 1970 when he was elected as a member of the national assembly of Pakistan. During the liberation movement he was a member of the Provisional Government of Bangladesh in exile.

KHAIRAT HUSAIN (1911-1972). A founding member of the Awami
League (q.v.). He participated as a member of the Muslim
League (q.v.) in the Lahore Convention of the Muslim League
in 1940 which called for a separate state for the Muslims of India. For his support of the language movement, he was jailed
by the government of Pakistan for a period of 18 months. During
the first martial law era in Pakistan he was placed under custody.
In 1962 he established the National Democratic Front. In 1970
he served as the secretary of the Pakistan National League which
was established by Ataur Rahman Khan (q.v.).

KHALIQUZZAMAN, CHAUDHURY (1889-1973). A Muslim League (q.v.)
politician from the United Provinces (now Uttar Pradesh) where
he gained prominence. He migrated to Pakistan in 1948 and succeeded Jinnah (q.v.) as president of the Muslim League later
that year. He was governor of East Bengal, 1953-1954.

KHALJI, IKHTIYARUDDIN MUHAMMAD BAKHTIYAR (d. 1206). A
leader in the army of the Slave dynasty of the Delhi sultanate.
He defeated the last Sena (q.v.) king in 1202 at Nadia and
brought Bengal under the control of the sultanate. His later
excursion through Assam toward Tibet ended in failure in 1205.

KHAN, ABUL KASEM (b. 1905). Heads the largest Bangladeshi industrial establishment. The A. K. Khan group was the only
indigenous East Pakistani group ranked in the 30 largest Pakistani
industrial, commercial and financial houses in the 1960s. After
Bangladeshi independence many holdings were nationalized during
the regime of Sheikh Mujibur Rahman (q.v.), but the group has
remained important and some properties were returned during the
regime of H. M. Ershad (q.v.). A. K. Khan himself was a minister from 1958 to 1962 in the Ayub Khan (q.v.) regime.

KRISHAK PRAJA PARTY (KPP) (Peasants' and People's Party). The
political vehicle of Fazlul Haq (q.v.) before Indian independence.
It was founded in 1927 and formally structured prior to the 1937
elections. Intended to be noncommunal, it, in fact, received
little non-Muslim support. The KPP found its base among
the peasants, principally in eastern Bengal, and it opposed the
landlord system. The difficulty was that the restrictive franchise
rules made most of the peasants, many of them tenants, ineli-
gible to vote. The KPP also opposed the landlord-dominated
Muslim League (q.v.). The party won about one-third of the
seats in the Bengal legislative assembly, but was able to form a
coalition with the Muslim League and govern Bengal until 1941.
The Muslim League withdrew in that year, but the KPP joined
with non-Congress Hindus and others and continued in office
until 1943. At that time, a Muslim League-led ministry replaced
it. In the 1945 election the party did poorly although Fazlul
Haq retained his seat. The party disappeared at the time of independence in 1947. Haq, however, formed the Krishak Sramik
Party (KSP) (q.v.) after independence.

KRISHAK SRAMIK PARTY (KSP) (peasants' and workers' party). A
revival by Fazlul Haq (q.v.) of the Krishak Praja Party (KPP)
(q.v.). Fazlul Haq became advocate general of East Bengal
briefly after independence, but had temporarily dropped out of
party politics. With the approach of the election to the provincial asembly in 1954, he returned to active politics and formed
the KSP. The party continued to champion the cause of the
peasant who had, in many cases, gained ownership of his land
through zamindari abolition. Also, this election, unlike preindependence elections, would be held under universal franchise.
The KSP joined with the Awami League (q.v.) in the United Front
(q.v.) which trounced the Muslim League (q.v.) in the election.
The KSP leader was chosen as the first chief minister under the
United Front, but Fazlul Haq was soon ousted from office by the
central government. With the revival of the assembly in 1956,
Abu Hussain Sarkar (q.v.) of the Krishak Sramik Party became
chief minister, but the United Front had divided and Sarkar and
Ataur Rahman Khan (q.v.) of the Awami League alternated chief
ministerships until martial law was imposed in October 1958.
Fazlul Haq died in 1962, at about the same time that party activity was again permitted. A KSP continued to exist after his
death, but it has been a small, unimportant group.

- L -

LAHORE RESOLUTION. Passed March 23, 1940, by the Muslim League.
It is often called, incorrectly, the Pakistan resolution; the word
Pakistan does not appear in the document. The resolution stated
that, if conditions for the Muslims of India did not improve, the
League would have no alternative but to call for the creation of
independent states in the eastern and northwestern Indian areas
which had a Muslim majority in the population. The plural "states"
was used in 1940, with the implication that there would not be a
single Muslim state. At a meeting of Muslim League (q.v.)
legislators, this was modified in 1946 and the singular "state"
was used and a single state was created by the partition of India
in 1947. Fazlul Haq (q.v.) was among the movers of the resolution; Suhrawardy (q.v.) supported the alteration in 1946.

LALAN SHAH (d. 1890). Folk poet and composer. His poetry and
songs are considered as treasures of Bengali literature. An
annual festival of music and poetry is still held in Bangladesh.

LAND FRAGMENTATION. This phenomenon results primarily from
Islamic inheritance rules. In the usual pattern, on the death of
a landholder the land is divided among his children, with sons
receiving a full share and daughters a half share. As the land
inherited is not of uniform quality, an effort is made to share the
land so that each inheritor will receive shares of the best, the
middling and the poorest land. The outcome is that an heir may

receive three or four or more small parcels of land as an inheritance. The result over several generations is evident. Government data (1977 agricultural census) indicate that most holdings contain six to nine fragments, and about 10 percent contain 20 or more. The average holding (of those who owned land) was 3.5 acres; if the landless are included in the calculation, the average holding is only 2.3 acres.

LAND REFORM. The Permanent Settlement (q.v.) of 1793 converted tax-farmers into landowners (zamindars). Most land in Bengal was owned by zamindars (often absentee) and most tillers were either share-cropping tenants or landless laborers. After Pakistani independence, in 1951, an East Bengal land reform act was passed that limited holdings of a cultivating family to 100 bighas (33 acres). In September 1984, the Ershad regime decreed a new land reform ordinance under which the maximum permissible holding was reduced generally to 60 bighas (20 acres). Surplus land would be distributed to the landless and to very small holders, but the amount of surplus land was estimated at less than half a million acres. In the 1977 agricultural census, it was reported that only 0.4 percent of farmers held more than 25 acres. See also land fragmentation.

LANGUAGE. Bangladesh is, for all practical purposes, a unilingual nation and is therefore unique among the nations of South Asia. All primary and much secondary and higher education is in Bengali. The language is a member of the Sanskritic (or Indic) branch of the Indo-European family and has developed a strong literary tradition (see, e.g., Tagore and Nazrul Islam). Other languages used in Bangladesh include English, Urdu and several tribal languages.

LEGAL FRAMEWORK ORDER. Issued by Pakistani President Yahya Khan (q.v.) in 1970 to set parameters for the operation of that constituent assembly to be elected in December of that year. The principal points were: (1) a federal state; (2) Islamic principles would be paramount; (3) direct and regular elections; (4) fundamental rights guaranteed; (5) independent judiciary; (6) maximum provincial autonomy, "but the federal government shall also have adequate powers, including legislative, administrative and financial powers, to discharge its responsibilities;" and (7) disparities between the provinces will be removed. The order was in major part a response to the six points (q.v.) of Mujibur Rahman (q.v.). The major conflict in the two documents is between Yahya's sixth and Mujib's fourth, in which the latter stated that all power of taxation would be at the provincial level and the provinces would grant sums to the federal government to carry out its duties.

LIAQUAT ALI KHAN (1895-1951). Although from a prominent east Punjab family, he gained his political experience in the United

Provinces (now Uttar Pradesh, India). He served in the provincial legislative bodies, 1926-1940, and in the Central Legislative Assembly, from 1940 until its dissolution in 1947, and was leader of the Muslim League (q.v.) group in that body. He was also a member for finance in the interim cabinet, 1946-1947. Liaquat was Jinnah's (q.v.) principal lieutenant as general secretary of the League from 1936 until independence, when he became prime minister. He was assassinated in Rawalpindi on October 16, 1951.

LOCAL GOVERNMENT. In Bangladesh is based on the zilla (district) system established by the Mughals. The British retained the system. At the time of independence in 1971 there were 18 districts in East Pakistan clustered into four divisions (Chittagong, Dhaka, Khulna and Rajshahi). The districts were divided into subdivisions (upazillas) and these in turn into thanas (literally, the area under a police station). Below these were unions, usually containing several hamlets or villages. There is no formal governmental system for the hamlets or villages. The Ershad government has changed the system somewhat: the former districts are now designated regions with powers so far undetermined. The former subdivisions are now designated districts. Areas roughly equivalent to thanas are now termed upazillas. The division at the top and the union at the bottom are unchanged. There are four divisions, 20 regions, 64 districts, 460 upazillas and 4,354 unions under the present system. There are to be elected councils at each level with the union council attending to local affairs and the upazilla council to serve as the main locus for development and coordination. The stated reason for the change was to bring development decision-making closer to the people.

- M -

MAHASTHAN GARH. An archeological site in the district of Bogra, is identified with the Pundranagar mentioned in the records of the Mauya empire and the Gupta, Pala and Sena dynasties. This old ruined city is situated near the Korotoya River. The city is surrounded by 11-foot thick defense walls 500 feet long on two sides and 450 feet on the other two sides. Excavations have resulted in the discoveries of copper, bronze and gold jewelry, pendants, badges and coins. This area was later conquered by Muslim generals. It is the site of the Mazar (grave) of Saint Shah Sultan Baki Mahisawar.

MAINAMATI. Five miles outside of Comilla town, contains the archeological sites of Mainamati and Lalmai. These two sites are thought to be the remains of the one-time political and cultural center of this region. Excavations show that the structures spread along a ridge for a distance of 11 miles. The structures are Buddhist monasteries and stupas often inset with characteristic terracotta plaques. They date from as early as the 7th century.

MAJORS. Refers to the leaders of the August Coup (q.v.) of 1977. They were Lt. Colonel Syed Farook Rahman and Majors Shariful Huq Dalim, Abdur Nur Choudhury, Abdul Hafiz, Badrul Rashid and M. Huda. After they were ousted in November 1977, they, along with a number of other officers, were forced to leave the country. Some of them were later permitted to join the Bangladesh foreign service. Two other coup attempts are linked to this group, including the Bogra Mutiny (q.v.). Lt. Colonel Syed Farook Rahman returned to Bangladesh and in 1986 he contested the presidential election won by Lt. General H. M. Ershad (q.v.).

MAJUMDAR, PHANI BHUSHAN (1901-1981). A follower of Subash Chandra Bose was a member of the Revolutionary Political Party from 1930-1938. He spent a considerable amount of time in jail during the British era in India. He was elected a member of the East Bengal Legislative Assembly in 1954. From 1954 until 1962 he was under arrest by the Pakistani government. In 1970, as an Awami League nominee, he was elected as a member of the Pakistan National Assembly. During the liberation war, he was a member of the advisory board of the Provisional Bangladesh Government-in-exile. He was a member of the cabinets of Mujibur Rahman (q.v.) and Mustaque Ahmed (q.v.), 1972-1975.

MALIK, ABDUL MUTTALIB (1905-1977). Appointed governor of East Pakistan by Yahya Khan (q.v.) in November 1971, during the civil war, in an attempt to civilianize the embattled Pakistani regime. He had earlier been appointed a minister in the central government by Yahya in 1969. An ophthalmologist by training, he had entered politics as a member of the Bengal legislature (1936-1947). After Pakistan's independence he served as a cabinet minister and as ambassador to a number of countries. He played no role in independent Bangladesh.

MAMUN MAHMUD (1929-1971). Entered the Police Service in 1947. He served as Superintendent of Police in Chittagong and Khulna. He was also the Deputy Inspector General, Rajshahi. He raised the black flag of protest on March 4, 1971, against the military rule of President Yahya Khan (q.v.). On March 26, 1971, a day after the beginning of the civilian massacre by the Pakistan army, he was called by a Brigadier Abdullah and was never heard from again.

MANSUR ALI (1919-1975). Assassinated during the Dhaka jail killing (q.v.), was the last Prime Minister of Bangladesh during the presidency of Sheikh Mujibur Rahman (q.v.). He was also the General Secretary of BAKSAL (q.v.). A lawyer by profession, he was elected three times as the President of the Pabna Lawyers

Association. He was a Vice-President of the Pabna District Muslim League from 1946 to 1950. He joined the Awami League (q.v.) in 1951 and had his first ministerial appointment in 1956 in Ataur Rahman Khan's (q.v.) cabinet. In 1969 he became the Vice-President of the Awami League. He served as the finance minister in the Provisional Bangladesh Government-in-exile. After the independence of Bangladesh and before he became Prime Minister in 1975, he served in a number of ministries including Commerce, Finance and Industries.

MANZUR, MUHAMMAD ABUL Major-General (1940-1981). Awarded Bir Uttam for bravery during the war of liberation. He is said to have been one of the leaders of the coup attempt which led to the assassination of President Ziaur Rahman (q.v.) in May 1981. Following the failure of the coup he was arrested and killed. In 1957 he joined the Pakistan Army and by 1971 was a Brigade Commander. During the war of liberation he escaped from Pakistan and actively participated in the war as a Sector Commander. In 1973, he became the military attaché of Bangladesh in New Delhi, India. He later became the Chief of the General Staff of the Bangladesh Army. In 1977 he became the General Officer, Commander of the 24th Division based in Chittagong. He was G.O.C. 24th Division when he became involved in the coup attempt. He was first a friend and later a foe of President Ziaur Rahman.

MARTIAL RACES. A term introduced by the British following the mutiny of the Bengal Army in 1857. The Bengal Army was comprised mainly of soldiers (sepoys) recruited from the lower Ganges basin. The British were aided in quelling the rebellion by Sikh and Muslim Punjabi troops and some other groups from northern India. After the end of the mutiny the British determined to recruit only from those areas that had supported them; these peoples were designated "martial races" and included the Punjabis. The peoples of the former recruiting grounds in the lower Ganges basin were described as "non-martial races," and were not recruited. The designations continued to operate in practice to a large degree even after Pakistani independence and resulted in an army in which the Bengalis were very much under-represented.

MARTYRS' DAY. Celebrated annually on February 21, it honors those who lost their lives during the language movement to make Bengali a national language of Pakistan. The incident occurred on February 21, 1952, when police fired upon students demonstrating against the plan to make Urdu the national language of Pakistan. A number of students were killed as a result of the police firing. The firing took place near the Dhaka Medical College and a monument has been erected near the place where the students were killed. It is called the Shahid Minar.

MASHIUR RAHMAN (1928-1979). A prominent parliamentarian, started
his political career as a member of the Muslim League (q.v.).
In 1957, he joined the National Awami Party (q.v.) and became
a leading member of the organization. He was a member of the
Pakistan National Assembly in 1962 and deputy leader of the
opposition. He was again elected to the National Assembly in
1965 but resigned in 1969 when the movement to oust President
Ayub started. He became the general secretary of the East
Pakistan National Awami party. During the war of liberation he
first left for India but later surrendered to the Pakistani armed
forces and opposed the liberation forces. After the liberation
of Bangladesh, he was arrested as a traitor but was later released. After the death of Maulana Bhashani (q.v.), he became
the leader of the National Awami Party in 1977. During the presidency of Ziaur Rahman (q.v.), his faction of the National Awami
Party joined the Bangladesh Nationalist Party (q.v.) and he became the only senior minister of Ziaur Rahman's cabinet and minister of railways. In the 1979 election he was elected as a member of the parliament once again. It was believed that he would
be the prime minister, but he died suddenly just before the
cabinet was announced. Shah Azizur Rahman (q.v.) became the
prime minister in his stead.

MIDDLE EAST. Relations between Bangladesh and most nations in
the Middle East did not exist prior to the Lahore meeting of the
Islamic Conference (q.v.) when several of the Arab delegates
persuaded Pakistan (q.v.) to invite Bangladesh to the meeting.
Thereafter, during the early part of the Zia regime, most Middle
Eastern countries recognized Bangladesh and established formal
diplomatic relations. Several countries, especially Kuwait and
Saudi Arabia, have provided economic assistance to Bangladesh.
Many countries also serve as hosts to Bangladeshi labor. This
has generated as much as $500 million per year in remittances to
Bangladesh. There have also been objections by some Middle
Eastern countries, notably Saudi Arabia, to the principle of
secularism contained in the Bangladeshi constitution (see Mujibbad). This provision was modified by Zia to provide for Muslims in Bangladesh being enabled to order their lives in ac-
cordance with the Sunna while retaining provisions allowing
freedom of religion.

MINTO, GILBERT JOHN ELLIOT-MURRAY-KYNYNMOUND, 4TH EARL
OF (1845-1914). The viceroy of India, 1905-1910. (He was
great-grandson of the 1st earl who was viceroy, 1806-1813.)
Minto was governor general of Canada, 1898-1904. He was required to restore the authority of the office of governor general
which had been lowered in the dispute between his predecessor,
Lord Curzon (q.v.), and the commander-in-chief, Lord Kitchener.
He was successful in doing this. Minto came to office at a time
when changes in the constitutional arrangements for India were
imminent. He worked with Lord Morley, the secretary of state

for India, in framing the Government of India Act of 1909 (q.v.).
A key aspect of this was the question of separate electorates
(q.v.) for Muslims. Minto received a Muslim delegation headed
by the Aga Khan (q.v.) at Simla in 1906. The delegation
pressed for separate electorates. They were incorporated into
the 1909 act.

MIR JAFAR (d. 1765). Remains a symbol for treachery in Bengal.
He was a brother-in-law of Alivardi Khan (q.v.) and played his
treachery on Alivardi's grandson and successor, Sirajuddaulah
(q.v.). At the battle of Plassey (q.v.) in 1757 between Sirajuddaulah and the British under Clive (q.v.), Mir Jafar deserted
Sirajuddaulah contributing to the latter's defeat. Mir Jafar was
rewarded with becoming governor of Bengal himself, but was
soon displaced (in 1760) by his son-in-law, Mir Qasim (q.v.), at
the instance of the British. Mir Jafar returned to the governor's
post in 1764.

MIR QASIM (died after 1764). A son-in-law and successor as governor of Bengal to Mir Jafar (q.v.) and was in turn succeeded by
Mir Jafar. He was installed as governor in 1760 at the instance
of the British at the same time ceding the districts of Chittagong,
Midnapur and Burdwan to the East India Company. His actions
to curb the private trade of British Company officers led to a
worsening of relations between Mir Qasim and the Company. He
is said to have perpetrated a massacre of British at Patna. In
1764, the British attacked Mir Qasim. He was defeated at the
battle of Buxar on October 22, 1764. Mir Qasim fled and died
in poverty in Delhi about 1770.

MIRZA, ISKANDAR (1899-1969). A collateral of the family of the
nawabs of Murshidabad (q.v.), was in 1919 the first Indian cadet
to graduate from Sandhurst, but served his career primarily in
the Indian Political Service. After independence he was defense
secretary (1947-1954), governor of East Bengal (1954), a central
minister (1954-1955) and governor general (1955-1956). He then
became the first president of Pakistan in 1956. In October 1958,
he ended parliamentary government and proclaimed martial law,
but was dismissed later than month by the chief martial law administrator, Ayub Khan (q.v.). He died in exile in London and
was buried in Tehran.

MOHAMMADULLAH. President of Bangladesh from January 1974 to
January 1975. After he stepped down from the presidency he
was the minister of Land Administration and Land Reform till
August 1975, when the regime of Mujibur Rahman (q.v.) was
overthrown.

MOHSIN, HAJI MOHAMMAD (1732-1812). A philanthropist and social
activist, was a life-long bachelor who withdrew from an active
life at age 32 and became a _fakir_ and in that capacity he visited

Egypt, Turkey, Iran and Saudi Arabia. In 1906 he donated all
of his property for the education of Muslims in India. He was
the founder of the Hooghly College in Calcutta and established
madarassa (religious schools) in Dhaka, Rajshahi and Chittagong.
He also established the Moshin Scholarship Fund for Higher Education of meritorious students. Today, when someone donates a
large sum, that person is called Haji Mohsin in honor of Haji
Mohammad Mohsin.

MONEM KHAN, ABDUL (1899-1971). A member of the Muslim League
since 1935, was the founder-secretary of the Mymensingh district
Muslim League. He was a member of the Constituent Assembly of
Pakistan till 1954. A protege of Nurul Amin (q.v.) he was a
mid-level political leader of East Pakistan who did not have the
stature or the personality of leaders such as A. K. Fazlul Haq
(q.v.) or H. S. Suhrawardy (q.v.). Nonetheless, he was a
shrewd politician who spoke the language of the people. Elected
as a member of the National Assembly of Pakistan in 1962, he
was brought to national limelight by President Ayub Khan (q.v.),
first as a central minister of Health, Labor and Social Welfare,
and then as Governor of East Pakistan, 1962-1969. He was assassinated in 1971, during the Bangladesh civil war.

MONI SINGH (b. 1901). Chairman of the Communist Party of Bangladesh (q.v.). His participation in anti-British movements and his
leadership in organizing the peasant movement brought him to
the forefront of politics. For these activities he was arrested
a number of times by the British. During the Pakistani period
he was also frequently under arrest. He was associated with
the freedom movement of Bangladesh and was a member of the
Consultative Committee of the Bangladesh Provisional Government-
in-Exile. After independence he cooperated with the Sheikh Mujibur Rahman (q.v.).

MONTAGU-CHELMSFORD ACT see GOVERNMENT OF INDIA ACT OF
1919

MORLEY-MINTO ACT see GOVERNMENT OF INDIA ACT OF 1909

MOTHAR HUSAIN, KAZI (1897-1981). Granted the title of National
Professor in 1975 for his contribution to science. In 1926 he
organized the Muslim Literature Society and became the President
of the Pakistan Literature Society in 1952.

MOUNTBATTEN OF BURMA, LOUIS MOUNTBATTEN, 1ST EARL (1900-
1979). The son of Prince Louis of Battenberg (later Mountbatten)
and Princess Victoria of Hesse (a granddaughter of Queen Victoria), was viceroy of India in 1947 and governor general of India, 1947-1948. His was the task of withdrawing British power
from India and (reluctantly) arranging for the partition of the
British dominions between India and Pakistan.

MUGHAL EMPIRE. The Mughal Empire (1526-1857) was the successor ruler in Delhi to the Delhi Sultanate (q.v.). Babar, the founder of the dynasty, defeated the last Lodi sultan at the battle of Panipat in 1526. The dominions of the Mughals soon spread from Afghanistan to Bengal and as far south as the Deccan. The principal rulers were the first six: Babar (1526-1530), Humayun (1530-1540 and 1555-1556), Akbar (1556-1605), Jahangir (1605-1627), Shahjahan (1627-1658), and Aurangzeb (1658-1707). Thereafter, the dynasty declined and was, in effect, under British control from the early 19th century until the final collapse in 1857 following the mutiny. With respect to Bengal, control was taken by the Mughals under Humayun in 1538, but was lost a year later to Sher Shah Suri (q.v.) whose descendants ruled Bengal until 1564. A short non-Mughal period followed until 1576 when the Mughals regained control under Akbar. Mughal governors ruled from Murshidabad (q.v.) and in 1765 the emperor Shah Alam II granted the diwani (q.v.) to the British.

MUJIBBAD (Mujibism). The term used for the four pillars espoused by Sheikh Mujibur Rahman (q.v.) as the key principles on which the government of independent Bangladesh would be based: nationalism, secularism, socialism and democracy. They are part of the 1972 constitution. Mujibbad follows closely the four principles attributed to Jawaharlal Nehru of India: democracy, socialism, secularism and non-alignment.

MUJIBUR RAHMAN, SHEIKH (1921-1975). Prime minister (1972-1975) and president (1975) of Bangladesh. He began his political career as a student in Calcutta in 1940 with the Muslim Students' Federation, an arm of the Muslim League (q.v.). He was a founding member with Husain Shahid Suhrawardy (q.v.) of the Awami League (q.v.) in 1949. He was the principal organizer of the party in East Bengal, later East Pakistan. He was minister of commerce in East Pakistan, 1956-1957, but was best respected for his party organizational abilities rather than for his administrative skills, a factor which would make his management of Bangladesh difficult.

After Suhrawardy's death in 1963, Mujib became de facto national leader of the Awami League, although his official position pertained only to East Pakistan. In this role, he proclaimed the Six-Point Program (q.v.) in 1966. He led the Awami League to an overwhelming victory in the 1970 elections in East Pakistan, but his party was unable to win any seats in West Pakistan. Following the negotiations among Mujib, Bhutto (q.v.) and Yahya Khan (q.v.) in early 1971, Mujib came under increasing pressure to declare independence, rather than autonomy within Pakistan, as the goal of the Awami League. When the army took action in March 1971, Mujibur Rahman was arrested and held in West Pakistan until after the surrender of the Pakistan army in East Pakistan. Much of this time was spent under the threat of death, but Bhutto, who replaced Yahya Khan after the defeat, released

Mujib and permitted him to return to Bangladesh. He arrived
in January 1972, and assumed the prime ministership. Under
his leadership the parliament enacted a constitution which called
for a parliamentary system and embraced what came to be called
Mujibbad (q.v.). However, the administration was very poorly
run and, under increasing opposition, he obtained parliamentary
approval for a presidential system with himself as president in
January, 1975. In June, 1975, he dissolved the Awami League
into BAKSAL (q.v.) which became the only legal party in
Bangladesh. Mujib was assassinated by disgruntled army officers
on August 15, 1975.

MUKTI BAHINI. Literally means freedom force. It was initially an
ad hoc fighting force formed after the beginning, in March 1971,
of military operations against the civilian population of Bangladesh by units of the Pakistani army. It was mainly composed
of Bengali personnel serving in the Pakistani army, the East
Bengal Regiment, the East Pakistan Police, and civilians who took
arms against the Pakistani army. The Mukti Bahini received Indian assistance in small arms and training. Some members of
the Mukti Bahini were incorporated into the Jatiyo Rakkhi Bahini
(q.v.) after independence.

MURSHED, SYED MAHBUB (1911-1979). A nephew of A. K. Fazlul
Haq (q.v.), was a barrister who became a judge in 1955 and
chief justice in 1964 of the Dhaka High Court. He resigned in
1968 to enter politics and was a member of the Democratic Action
Committee (q.v.) that negotiated with Ayub Khan (q.v.) in 1969.
Murshed announced himself a candidate for the presidency for
the election in 1969, a poll which was not held.

MURSHIDABAD. A city on the Bhagirathi River in West Bengal.
Founded in 1704 by Murshid Quli Zafar Khan, it was at first only
the headquarters of the Diwan. As he rose from Diwan to Nawab
of Bengal, Murshidabad became the capital of Bengal till 1773.
Murshidabad is separated from Bangladesh by the river Padma.
A number of prominent Bengali Muslim families come from Murshidabad (q.v., e.g., Iskandar Mirza).

MUSHARAF HUSAIN, NAWAB (1871-1966). A businessman, politician
and philanthropist, was given the title of Nawab in 1926. In 1918
he was a member of the Bengal Legislative Council and became
Education Minister of Bengal in 1927. He was responsible for
passing the first education bill in Bengal. He was a member of
the Fazlul Haq (q.v.) cabinet, 1937. He established a number of
schools and madarashas or religious schools.

MUSHARIF, KHALID (d. 1975). A Bengali major in the Pakistani
army in 1971, came to prominence as a hero during the war of
independence. He was an ambitious officer who was promoted to
brigadier by Sheikh Mujibur Rahman (q.v.). Pro-Indian in his

outlook, he masterminded the countercoup of November 3, 1977, which resulted in the ouster of majors who were responsible for the August Coup (q.v.). He himself was overthrown and killed by a popular uprising in the army on November 7, 1977.

MUSLIM LEAGUE. A political party founded in Dhaka in December 1906. Its initial goals were to support the Crown and to further the cause of the Muslims of India without opposing the other groups in India. Its founding followed the Simla meeting of Muslims with Lord Minto (q.v.). The Muslims demanded separate electorates (q.v.) for Muslims. This demand was met in the Government of India Act of 1909 (q.v.) and accepted by the Indian National Congress in an agreement with the Muslim League signed in 1916 at Lucknow. The League gained its most important member when Muhammad Ali Jinnah (q.v.) joined in 1913. He led the Muslim League negotiations with the Congress at Lucknow. The Congress soon repented of its acceptance of separate electorates and worked to end the system beginning in the 1920s up to partition in 1947. Jinnah agreed in 1928 to yield on the issue if other safeguards for the Muslim minority were given; this was not done by the Congress or the British. The League contested elections as a single body first in 1937. It did well in the Muslim-minority provinces but poorly in the Muslim-majority provinces. It was seen by many Bengali Muslims as the party of Calcutta Muslims and those Muslims who belonged to the national elite (q.v.). At a session of the League in Lucknow later in 1937, four of the Muslim prime ministers (including Fazlul Haq [q.v.]) agreed to support the League in national matters in return for a free hand in their own provincial affairs. This greatly strengthened Jinnah's position and that of the League.

On March 23, 1940, the Lahore Resolution (q.v.) was passed in which the possibility of a demand for partition was expressed. In the 1945 election the League won handsome majorities in the Muslim seats in all the Muslim-majority provinces except the Northwest Frontier Province. Jinnah took this as a mandate to press for partition. The demand was accepted and Pakistan was created on August 14, 1947. After independence and the death of Jinnah (1948), the League began to weaken. It was defeated badly in the election to the East Bengal provincial assembly in 1954 and shortly after split in West Pakistan.

All parties were banned by Ayub Khan (q.v.) when martial law was declared in October 1958. In 1962, Ayub resurrected the Pakistan Muslim League (Convention) (q.v.); some of his opponents formed the Council Muslim League (q.v.). Both parties did poorly in the 1970 election; neither won a seat in East Pakistan. In Bangladesh, since independence, the party was banned during the period of Mujibur Rahman (q.v.) but permitted to return during the period of Ziaur Rahman (q.v.). The party led by Abdul Sobur Khan (q.v.) won 20 seats in the 1979 parliamentary election, but has since splintered and is of small consequence. (See also Bangladesh Muslim League.)

MUSTAQUE AHMED, KHONDAKAR (b. 1918). President of Bangladesh
from August 1975 to November 1975. He is currently the President of Democratic League (q.v.). Active in the language movement, he was also a founding member of the Awami League (q.v.).
In 1954, he served as the chief whip of the United Front (q.v.)
government. During the 1969 political movement to oust President Ayub Khan (q.v.) he was the convenor of the East Pakistan
Democratic Action Committee (q.v.) and participated in the round
table conference held at that time. He was elected to the national assembly in 1970. During the liberation war, he was the
foreign minister and minister for law and parliamentary affairs
in the Bangladesh provisional government-in-exile. He was a
member of the cabinet of Mujibur Rahman, (q.v.) 1972-1975. He
became president of the country after Mujibur Rahman was assassinated, but gave up the presidency when a countercoup led
by Khaled Musharraf took place in November 1975. He was arrested in 1976 and released in 1980. He is characterized to be a
conservative, western oriented politician.

- N -

NATIONAL AWAMI PARTY (NAP) (National People's Party). Formed
in East Pakistan by Maulana Abdul Hamid Khan Bhashani (q.v.)
when he withdrew in 1957 from the Awami League (q.v.). Bhashani objected to the program of Suhrawardy (q.v.) which he
saw as too pro-Western and too market-economy oriented. Bhashani coalesced with several West Pakistani leaders of small parties which were either regional or leftist or both. In the 1960s,
the party split with one branch remaining with Bhashani (called
the NAP[B]) and often incorrectly referred to as "pro-China."
The other splinter was headed nationally by Khan Abdul Wali
Khan (the NAP[W]) and in East Pakistan by Muzaffar Ahmad
(q.v.). Both factions in East Pakistan failed to attract appre-
ciable support in the 1970 election. Since independence and especially since the death of Bhashani in 1976, the NAP(B) has
splintered many times and is all but nonexistent. Some members
even joined the Bangladesh Nationalist Party (q.v.), including
Mashiur Rahman (q.v.), the presumptive prime minister in 1979
(he died as the election results were coming in). The Muzaffar
Ahmad group, reinitialed NAP(M) after 1971, has also been of
little consequence since independence although winning an occa-
sional seat. Muzaffar strongly supported BAKSAL (q.v.) in
1975 as a means toward political survival.

NATIONAL ELITE. A term applied to those in Muslim Bengali leadership who tended to use Urdu as a family language (hence, they
are also known as the Urdu elite) rather than Bengali. This
distinguished them from the Hindu elite of Bengal but also had
several other consequences. The members were often descendants
of Mughal or Delhi sultanate officers who had been sent to Bengal

to govern and whose families remained in the region. Often,
they were also Muslim zamindars, e.g., the nawab of Dhaka
(q.v.). In the Muslim League (q.v.) they tended to support
national issues rather than Bengali issues. Among these were such
leaders as Nazimuddin (q.v.). Their use of Urdu detached them
from the mass of Bengalis and permitted such vernacular elite
(q.v.) leaders as Fazlul Haq (q.v.) to achieve prominence. After
Pakistan's independence this group continued to support the Muslim League even to the extent of supporting Urdu as the Pakistani
national language. Their power was destroyed in the East Bengal
election of 1954 in which the Muslim League was trounced by the
United Front (q.v.). To a limited degree, the national elite also
supported the Pakistan Muslim League (Convention) (q.v.) formed
by Ayub Khan (q.v.).

NATIONAL SOCIALIST PARTY   see   JATIYA SAMAJTANTRIK DAL

NAZIMUDDIN, KHWAJA (SIR) (1894-1964). A member of the nawab
family of Dhaka (q.v.). As a member of the legislative bodies
of Bengal, he served as a minister 1929-1934 and 1937-1941, the
latter under the premiership of A. K. Fazlul Haq (q.v.) during a
coalition between the Krishak Praja Party (q.v.) and the Muslim
League (q.v.). With the breakup of the coalition, Nazimuddin
became leader of the opposition, 1941-1943, but became prime minister in 1943, serving until the ministry was terminated by the
governor in 1945. After the 1946 elections he was denied a return to the premiership, as he was defeated by a rival Muslim
Leaguer, H. S. Suhrawardy (q.v.). However, after independence in 1947, he became chief minister of East Bengal, serving
until he was appointed in 1948 to succeed Muhammad Ali Jinnah
(q.v.) as governor general.
    When Liaqat Ali Khan (q.v.) was assassinated in 1951, Nazi-
muddin stepped down from the governor generalship to become
prime minister, remaining in office until he was dismissed in
1953 by Governor General Ghulam Muhammad (q.v.) although it
was not demonstrated that Nazimuddin had lost the confidence
of the constituent assembly. Nazimuddin remained a member,
though less active, of the constituent assembly and parliament
until the imposition of martial law in 1958. When political parties
were again permitted to function in 1962, he became president of
the Council Muslim League (q.v.) and was a leader of the Combined Opposition Parties (q.v.) in opposition to Ayub Khan
(q.v.) when he died in 1964. His brother, Khwaja Shahabuddin
(q.v.), was also prominent in politics. Although they were often
rivals, he, Fazlul Haq and Suhrawardy are buried in adjacent
graves in a Dhaka park.

NAZRUL ISLAM, KAZI (1893-1976). A Muslim poet whose principal
writings were done between 1919 and 1941. He opposed the
British rule in India and during the British period his writing
was frequently proscribed. He used legends and myths in his

poems. During the later part of his life, he was said to be
mentally unstable. Although he lived most of his life in Calcutta,
he moved to Bangladesh at the invitation of Sheikh Mujibur Rahman (q.v.).

NAZRUL ISLAM, SYED (1925-1975). Assassinated in the Dhaka jail
killings (q.v.). He was a close confidant of Sheikh Mujibur Rahman (q.v.) and headed the government-in-exile in 1971 when
Mujib was in jail in Pakistan. It was during his tenure as Minister of Industry that a large number of industries and banks
were nationalized. In 1975 he became the vice-president of Bangladesh. As a student leader he actively participated in the language movement. He joined the Awami League in 1953 and rose
through the ranks to be the senior vice president of the Awami
League.

NINETEEN-POINTS. A program outlined by Ziaur Rahman (q.v.)
in 1979. Zia provided, through the nineteen points, his ideas
of the direction that Bangladesh would be taking in economic,
political and social sectors. Affirming some fundamental constitutional principles as faith and reliance upon Allah, democracy, nationalism and socialism, he wanted to set up a self-reliant Bangladesh. Participation, food self-sufficiency, enhanced provision
of services including health and shelter, privatization and decentralization were some of the other program goals.

NIZAM-I-ISLAM. A small conservative Muslim political party established in 1953. It was said to have been influenced by A. K.
Fazlul Haq (q.v.). Nizam-i-Islam wanted a government based
on Islam and wanted separate electorate. This party joined the
United Front (q.v.) government in East Pakistan. It opposed
the martial law regime of President Ayub Khan (q.v.). During
the 1970s it did not support the Awami (q.v.) League-led Bangladesh freedom movement. After the independence of Bangladesh
it was banned. Nizam-i-Islam reemerged after the passing of
the Political Parties Regulation in 1976. It later merged with the
Islamic Democratic League (q.v.).

NOA MIA (1852-1883). Second son of Dudu Mia (q.v.), was named
Abdul Gaffar Noa Mia. In 1864 he became the leader of the
Faraizi movement. Like his father, he stressed religion rather
than politics or economics.

NOAKHALI. A district (now region) in southeastern Bangladesh
which became well known in 1946 when Mahatma Gandhi traveled
there to help relieve the communal violence that was occurring.
Gandhi achieved some success and then moved to other areas
including Calcutta (see Husain Shahid Suhrawardy) and Bihar to
attempt to accomplish the same results.

NOON, MALIK FIROZ KHAN (SIR) (1893-1970). A prominent Punjabi

political figure who held many positions in the Punjab government before independence, was Indian High Commissioner to London (1936-1941) and was a member of the Viceroy's council (1941-
1945). After independence, in addition to being a member of
the constituent assembly, he was governor of East Bengal, 1950-
1953, serving during some of the more difficult periods of the
Bengali language agitation. Noon, nonetheless, was popular per-
sonally and a school bearing his wife's name still operates in
Dhaka. He later was chief minister of the Punjab (1953-55),
foreign minister under Suhrawardy (q.v.) (1956-1957) and prime
minister (1958), until the imposition of martial law in October
1958.

NURUL AMIN (1897-1974). First entered the legislature as a member
of the Bengal Legislative Council in 1942, was elected to the Bengal Legislative Assembly in 1946 and was chosen speaker. At
independence he became a member of the Nazimuddin (q.v.)
cabinet in East Bengal and succeeded Nazimuddin as chief minister when the latter became governor general in 1948. Both he
and the Muslim League (q.v.) as a party were defeated in the
United Front (q.v.) sweep in the 1954 elections. He remained
leader of the Muslim League in East Pakistan until parties were
banned after the coup of Ayub Khan (q.v.) in 1958.
   In 1965, he was elected to the National Assembly as a member
of the National Democratic Front. In 1969, he played a prominent
role in the negotiations which ended with the resignation of Ayub
Khan. In 1970, as a candidate of the Pakistan Democratic Party,
he was one of only two non-Awami Leaguers elected to the National Assembly from East Pakistan. He strongly opposed the
separatist position taken by the Awami League in 1971 which led
to the breakup of Pakistan. He remained in Pakistan and became
vice-president in 1971 under Zulfiqar Ali Bhutto (q.v.), who
was president. He held the office until the parliamentary constitution of Pakistan took effect in 1973.

- O -

OSMANY, MUHAMMAD ATAUL GHANI (1918-1984). Commanded the
Mukti Bahini (q.v.) during the Bangladesh war of independence
in 1971. He had joined the British Indian army in 1939 and retired from the Pakistan army in 1967 with the rank of colonel.
He became active in politics, associating with the Awami League
(q.v.) and was elected to the National Assembly in the 1970 poll.
After the independence of Bangladesh, he was promoted to general
and made commander-in-chief of the Bangladesh army, a post
he held until April 1972. He then retired and returned to politics and was a member of the cabinet of Mujibur Rahman (q.v.).
In January 1975, he resigned his parliamentary seat in protest
to Mujibur Rahman's creation of BAKSAL (q.v.) as the sole party
in the country. Osmany in 1977 formed a separate party and in

1978 was the candidate of most of the opposition in the presidential election, standing against Ziaur Rahman (q.v.). Osmany was soundly defeated. He also ran for president in 1981, but not as a consensus opposition candidate, and again lost.

- P -

PAHARPUR. A Buddhist archeological site located near Rajshahi. This site, with its massive central Vihara (monastery) measuring about 350 yds. in diameter, is one of the largest such monasteries south of the Himalayas.

PAKISTAN. Relations between Pakistan and Bangladesh were, to say the least, strained after Bangladesh attained independence from Pakistan in December 1971. Pakistan proclaimed a doctrine under which it would break diplomatic relations with any state recognizing Bangladesh, a policy that became impractical when the major nations did so. Pakistan, with the aid of the veto of China (q.v.), kept Bangladesh from membership in the United Nations (q.v.). The Lahore summit of the Islamic Conference (q.v.) in 1974 began a reversal of this policy as Pakistan was persuaded by other Islamic countries to accept the fait accompli of Bangladeshi separation from Pakistan. Pakistan recognized Bangladesh and withdrew its opposition to Bangladeshi membership in the United Nations and other bodies, although the formal exchange of ambassadors did not occur until 1976.

Bangladesh and Pakistan as separate entities retain the fear of Hindu (now Indian) hegemony in South Asia that led Bengali Muslims to support so strongly the Pakistan concept in the 1946 election. The two countries cooperate in the Islamic Conference and in the South Asian Association for Regional Cooperation (q.v.) and often take identical positions on international issues (e.g., on Afghanistan and Kampuchea in opposition to India and on Palestine). One outstanding issue, the division of the assets and liabilities of united Pakistan, is unlikely ever to be resolved and has recently been ignored. Another issue is the continued presence of Biharis (q.v.) in Bangladesh who demand to be sent to Pakistan.

PAKISTAN DEMOCRATIC MOVEMENT. The term applied to a group of opposition parties that challenged the continued rule of Ayub Khan (q.v.). Most, but not all, opposition parties were formal members of the movement. However, other parties were also represented at the round table discussions in early 1969. These included the Pakistan People's Party of Zulfiqar Ali Bhutto (q.v.) and the Awami League (q.v.) led by Mujibur Rahman (q.v.).

PAKISTAN MUSLIM LEAGUE (CONVENTION). The name generally given to the political party formed to support Ayub Khan (q.v.). The name derived from a convention of Muslim Leaguers called by

Ayub following the 1962 elections to the national and provincial assemblies. Among the East Pakistanis who supported the Ayub League were Abdul Sobur Khan (q.v.) and Khwaja Shahabuddin (q.v.). Shahabuddin's brother, Nazimuddin (q.v.), supported the rival Council Muslim League (q.v.). Neither party won a seat in East Pakistan in the 1970 election.

PAKISTAN RESOLUTION see LAHORE RESOLUTION

PALA DYNASTY. Ruled Bengal from 750 to 1150. The dynasty received its name from all the rulers' names, which ended in "-pala." At its peak, the kingdom extended well into present-day Uttar Pradesh in India. The rulers were Buddhists and patronized the scholars of that religion.

PANNI, WAJID ALI KHAN (1869-1936). An educationist, philanthropist and social activist, belonged to the national elite (q.v.). He was a zamindar who was credited with establishing a number of educational institutions, small hospitals and dispensaries and building roads and canals. He participated in the Non-Cooperation movement against the British rule and was jailed for 15 months. His family has remained active in politics and administration. His sons Khurram Khan Panni and Humayun Khan Panni were legislators and ambassadors.

PARITY. A term associated with the constitution of Pakistan, 1956 (q.v.). East Pakistanis agreed to accept the equality (or parity) of membership in the national parliament, 150 members each from the east and west wings. This diluted the value of a vote from East Pakistan. The quid pro quo for this was that the government of Pakistan would commit itself to working for parity also in the administrative services and in the economy. Although steps were taken to try to redress the imbalance in the services, it was not possible to convince investors or to divert government investment funds to lessen the economic imbalance. Although the East Pakistani economy grew between 1956 and 1971, it grew at a slower rate than that of West Pakistan so that the disparity increased rather than decreased. The legislative parity was continued in Ayub Khan's (q.v.) constitution of Pakistan, 1962 (q.v.), but was discarded by Yahya Khan (q.v.) when he called for elections in 1970. At that time elections were held on a population basis: East Pakistan had 162 directly elected seats in the national assembly and West Pakistan had 138.

PEACE COMMITTEES. Set up in 1971 in various cities of Bangladesh and in localities within each city. The purpose of the committees was to persuade the Bangladeshis to accept the idea of maintaining a united Pakistan.

PERMANENT SETTLEMENT. Promulgated by Lord Cornwallis (q.v.) in 1793. Cornwallis designated the tax collectors (zamindars) as owners of the land from which they raised revenue. Previously these persons were, in effect, tax farmers who collected revenue from the farmers (<u>ryots</u>). With permanent settlement, the ryots became tenants of the zamindars. As it turned out, most, but not all, of the zamindars in eastern Bengal were Hindus. This led to challenges from such leaders as Fazlul Haq (q.v.) and his Krishak Praja Party (q.v.) in the 1930s. The system, however, was not changed until after the independence of Pakistan by land reform acts passed by the provincial assembly.

PLASSEY (Pilasi), BATTLE OF. Occurred on June 23, 1757. The battle was a showdown between the British under Clive (q.v.) and the governor of Bengal, Sirajuddaulah (q.v.). Aided by the treachery of Mir Jafar (q.v.), the British routed the Bengali force.

POPULATION PLANNING. One of the principal goals of the regimes of Ziaur Rahman (q.v.) and H. M. Ershad (q.v.) has been the reduction of the rate of population growth. The annual growth rate (1980-85) is 2.6 percent, indicating a growth from the current (1985) population of 101 million to 141 million in the year 2000, even if the projected decrease in the growth rate to 2.3 percent (1985-2000) occurs.

Bangladesh is the most densely populated country in the world (excluding the city states of Hong Kong and Singapore) with about 1,800 people per square mile. A population program was initiated in the 1950s and today there are family planning committees at every level of government. There has been but marginal success, partly owing to religious resistance and partly to earlier concentration on males. Current programs are more directed toward females.

- Q -

QUADRAT-E-KHUDA, MUHAMMAD TOFAZZIL (1900-1977). A prominent scientist who received 18 patents. Most of his patents are in the area of agricultural products. He served in a number of different capacities including being the first director of The Pakistan Scientific and Industrial Research Center. Soon after the independence of Bangladesh he was called to chair the first Educational Reform Committee. The report of the committee is known as the Quadrat-e-Khuda Education Commission report.

- R -

RAHMAN, HABIBUR (b. 1908). President of the Dhaka Muslim League and member of the Working Committee of the East Pakistan Muslim League between 1948-1950. He served as Pakistan's ambassador to a number of countries including Australia, New Zealand,

Switzerland, Belgium, Australia and Yugoslavia. During the
Ayub (q.v.) regime (1958-62) he served as Minister of Education, Information and Broadcasting and Minority Affairs. He
became a member of the National Assembly of Pakistan in 1962.

RAZZAKAR BAHINI. A force set up by the Pakistan army to counter
the Mukti Bahini (q.v.), mainly composed of pro-Pakistani Bengali and Biharis. The purpose of the force was to maintain
order. Members of the force gained a poor reputation because
they worked towards the suppression of the demands of the
Bangladeshi.

- S -

SALIMULLAH, NAWAB SIR (1866-1915). A social activist and a politician, known for his efforts to elevate the status of the Muslims
of India. He was the founder of both the Dhaka University and
the Ahsanullah Engineering College which is now the Bangladesh
Engineering University. He was one of the founders of the All
India Muslim League (see Muslim League). He supported Curzon
(q.v.) in the latter's decision to partition Bengal in 1905. A
number of organizations such as the Dhaka Orphanage, a medical
school, and a Dhaka University dormitory are named in his hon-
or.

SAMATATA. Mentioned in inscriptions of the second Gupta emperor,
Samudragupta (reigned c. 330-380 A.D.), as a kingdom in
eastern Bengal captured by him. Its capital is believed to have
been in the vicinity of present-day Comilla.

SARKAR, ABU HUSSAIN (1894-1969). Served as chief minister of
East Pakistan from 1955 to 1956 and again briefly in 1958. He
was a lawyer by profession. Arrested a number of times by the
British, he took part in the Swadeshi movement and in the national
movement for the independence of India. In 1935 he joined the
Krishak Praja Party (q.v.) of A. K. Fazlul Haq (q.v.) and as
representative of KPP was elected to the Bengal Legislative Assembly. As a nominee of the United Front (q.v.), he was
elected to the East Pakistan Legislative Assembly in 1954. He
also served as a central minister in 1955.

SATTAR, ABDUS (1906-1985). President of Bangladesh, 1981-1982,
had a career both in law and in politics. Associated with the
United Front (q.v.), he was appointed a minister in the Pakistan
government in 1956, a judge of the East Pakistan High Court in
1957, and a justice of the Pakistan Supreme Court in 1968. He
was also chief election commissioner and conducted the elections
of 1970 to the national and provincial assemblies. He was able
to flee Pakistan via Afghanistan in 1972 and held a number of
posts in Bangladesh. He became a special assistant to President

A. S. M. Sayem (q.v.) in 1975 and a minister, and in 1977
was appointed vice-president by President Ziaur Rahman (q.v.).
He succeeded Zia as acting president when the latter was assassinated on May 30, 1981, and was elected to the office on November 15, 1981. He was removed from the presidency by the
coup led by H. M. Ershad (q.v.) on March 24, 1982. He headed
JAGODAL (q.v.), founded in 1978 as a party to support Zia and
his program, and its successor, the Bangladesh Nationalist Party
(BNP) (q.v.), until 1979 when, with a parliament in office, Zia
assumed the chairmanship himself.

SAYEM, ABU SADAT MUHAMMAD (b. 1916). Became the President
of Bangladesh in November 1975, when a compromise took place
between Khalid Musharif (q.v.) and Khondakar Mustaque Ahmed
(q.v.) over who should lead Bangladesh. Sayem, who was the
chief justice at that time, was chosen. He was a lawyer by profession who spent a considerable amount of time at the bar.
While president, he held a number of important ministries including defense and foreign affairs. He was also Chief Martial
Law Administrator until November 1976. He relinquished his
presidency in April 1977.

SAYYID DYNASTY. Ruled Bengal from 1490 to 1538, when the region
was incorporated into the territories of the Mughal empire. The
dynasty was founded by Alauddin Hussain Shah (q.v.). It is
not to be confused with the Sayyid dynasty of the Delhi sultanate
which ruled from 1414 to 1451.

SEN, SURJA (1893-1934). A revolutionary who was hanged by the
British because of his anti-British activities, is noted for his
organization of the Chittagong armory raid of 1930. He formed
his revolutionary group towards the end of World War I and for
a time joined in the Non-Cooperation Movement of Mahatma Gandhi.
By 1923 he was disenchanted with nonviolence and began his radical movement, which included the attempt to murder a British
judge. He was in prison from 1926 to 1928 and in 1930 served
as the secretary of the Chittagong District Congress. He was
betrayed in 1933, was arrested by the British and hanged in
1934.

SENA DYNASTY. Ruled Bengal from about 1095 to 1245, succeeding
after consolidating the domains of the Pala dynasty (q.v.). Unlike the Palas, the Senas were Brahmanical Hindus who perhaps
set the stage for the rapid conversion of many in eastern Bengal
to Islam, a casteless religion as is the Buddhism the people once
espoused. The dynasty's end began with the conquest of Nadia
by Ikhtiyaruddin Muhammad Bakhtiyar Khalji (q.v.) in 1202. The
rulers retreated to eastern Bengal but were defeated in the next
half century and all of Bengal came under Muslim rule.

SEPARATE ELECTORATES. A system of voting under which members of each (religious) community would vote separately for representatives of their own community in legislative bodies. The Muslims demanded this system in a meeting at Simla with Lord Minto (q.v.) in 1906. The concept was included in the Government of India Act of 1909 (q.v.) and was accepted in an agreement between the Muslim League (q.v.) and the Congress at Lucknow in 1916. It remained an item high on the League agenda throughout the preindependence period. After independence, India abolished separate electorates. Pakistan continued to use the system until the indirect elections of the Ayub Khan (q.v.) period were held. Independent Bangladesh has not used separate electorates, but they had been revived in Pakistan under Zia ul-Haq. In changes after 1909, several other groups gained separate representation including Sikhs and Indian Christians. The opposite of separate electorates is described as joint electorates.

SERNIABAT, ABDUR RAB (d. 1975). A lawyer and a politician, was a member of the National Awami Party (q.v.) of Maulana Bhashani (q.v.). He joined the Awami League in 1969 and became a minister in the Provisional Government of Bangladesh in exile. After independence he became the Minister for Land Reform and Irrigation. A close relative of Sheikh Mujibur Rahman (q.v.), he was assassinated at the same time Mujib lost his life.

SHAH JALAL, HAZRAT (1271-1347). A religious preacher and soldier, was born in Turkey in 1271 and educated in Mecca. Reference to his death in 1347 was made by Ibn Batuta. In 1303 he conquered Sylhet after having fought Gaur Govind. He preached in Sylhet for 30 years and built a mosque which is in use today. A number of legends are associated with him, including the story that he crossed a river on his prayer rug in order to defeat Gaur Govind. His burial place in Sylhet is a pilgrimage site.

SHAHA, RONANDA PRASAD (1896-1971). A well-known social activist and philanthropist. He was a successful businessman who was initially involved in the supply of coal. He later expanded his business to include shipping, insurance and jute. In 1938 he set up a 20-bed hospital and a residential girls' school. Both these enterprises are well known throughout Bangladesh. During the great famine in Bengal in the early 1940s he donated generously to the Red Cross and maintained 250 free kitchens. After 1947, he chose to remain in Pakistan and was a leading member of the Hindu community. He and his only son were killed by the Pakistani army some time in 1971. The now much larger hospital at Mirzapur in the Tangail region remains a monument to the Shaha family.

SHAHABUDDIN, JUSTICE (1895-1969). Governor of East Bengal, 1954-1955. A south Indian Muslim from Mysore state, he entered the civil service in 1921 and rose to the position of chief justice of East Bengal. After serving as governor, he became a justice of the Supreme Court and chief justice for a brief period in 1960.

SHAHABUDDIN, KHWAJA (1898-1977). A member of the nawab of Dhaka family (q.v.) and younger brother of Khwaja Sir Nazimuddin (q.v.), had a long career of government service, often in the shadow of his elder brother. He was a member of the Bengal Legislative Assembly, 1937-1946, and a member of the Nazimuddin cabinet, 1943-1945. He served as governor of the Northwest Frontier Province, 1951-1954, and a member of the central cabinet, 1954-1955, and then undertook a number of diplomatic assignments. He returned to the central cabinet as minister of information under Ayub Khan, 1965-1969, thereby supporting a regime which was opposed by Nazimuddin. During this term of office he angered East Pakistanis by banning the works of Sir Rabindranath Tagore (q.v.) from Pakistan radio and television. After Bangladeshi independence, Shahabuddin stayed in Pakistan until his death.

SHAHIDULLAH, DR. MOHAMMAD (1885-1969). Considered the foremost educationist of his times. He served in a number of educational institutions including Calcutta, Dhaka and Rajshahi universities. He is credited with writing more than 25 books, including Essays on Islam, Traditional Culture in East Pakistan, and Hundred Sayings of the Holy Prophet.

SHARIATULLAH, HAJI (1779-1840). The founder of the Faraizi movement (q.v.), he studied in Mecca and returned to Bengal after 20 years. While there he studied Wahhabi principles and practices. Upon his return, he began the movement based on his Islamic beliefs. The essential principles of the movement were (1) political and economic freedom for peasants and workers, (2) protection of peasants and workers from the suppression of the zamindars, proprietors and those who were involved in the cultivation of indigo, (3) redirection of people from forms of worship which included such "un-Islamic practices as veneration of saints," and (4) avoidance of performing such important Islamic practices as the Friday prayers or the Eid prayers in India until India became a Muslim society. See also Kabir family.

SHEIKH HASINA WAJID (b. 1947). The daughter of Sheikh Mujibur Rahman (q.v.). She was absent in India on August 15, 1975, when the coup took place that took the lives of her father and many other members of the family. She returned to Bangladesh in 1979 to assume the leadership of the Awami League (q.v.). In 1986, she was elected to parliament and became the leader of the opposition.

SHER SHAH SURI (1472-1545). Rebelled against the Mughal emperor Humayun in 1539 and established himself as emperor of India

until his death in 1545. His successors continued to rule north
India until 1556, when Humayun reclaimed the throne. His
descendants then continued to rule independently in Bengal until 1564.

SIRAJ SIKDAR (1944-1975). A civil engineer by profession, he became involved with the labor movement in 1968. He was a member of the Communist Party and was a student leader. In June
1971 he formed the East Bengal Sarvohara (Proletariat) Party
which propagated a radical philosophy. He argued that East
Pakistan was a colony of West Pakistan and similarly that Bangladesh was a colony of India. He called for the overthrow of the
Sheikh Mujibur Rahman (q.v.) by force. He went underground
in 1974 but was arrested and killed by the Jatiyo Rakkhi Bahani
(q.v.) in 1975.

SIRAJUDDAULAH (c. 1737-1757). Governor of Bengal from April
1756 to June 1757. He succeeded his grandfather, Alivardi Khan
(q.v.). In June 1756, he attacked Calcutta and was held responsible for the incident of the Black Hole. The British sought
revenge. Subverting officers on Sirajuddaulah's side, including
Mir Jafar (q.v.), the British defeated Sirajuddaulah at the Battle
of Plassey (q.v.) on June 23, 1757. Sirajuddaulah was captured
and executed.

SIX-POINTS. A plan for the accommodation of the grievances of
East Pakistan put forward by Sheikh Mujibur Rahman (q.v.) in
1966. It became the platform of the Awami League (q.v.) in the
1970 elections. The six points were (1) federal parliamentary
government, with free and regular elections; (2) federal government to control only foreign affairs and defense; (3) a separate
currency or separate fiscal accounts for each province to control
movement of capital from east to west; (4) all power of taxation
at the provincial level, with the federal government subsisting on
grants; (5) each federating unit could enter into foreign trade
agreements on its own and control the foreign exchanged earned;
and (6) each unit could raise its own militia. These points
are based on the twenty-one point (q.v.) program of the United
Front (q.v.) in 1954. Yahya Khan (q.v.) issued a legal framework order (q.v.) prior to the 1970 elections, which was a response and a challenge to several of the points (see Legal Framework Order for a discussion of this).

SOBUR KHAN, ABDUL (1910-1982). A political leader associated
with the Muslim League (q.v), was a minister in the Ayub Khan
(q.v.) government, 1962-1969. After Bangladeshi independence
in 1971, the Muslim League was banned, but the party was permitted to return to political activity in 1976. As the leader of
the Bangladesh Muslim League (q.v.), Sobur was elected to parliament in 1979.

SONARGAON. The first seat of the Pala dynasty which ruled Bengal from the 7th to the 10th centuries. This archeological site has a number of monuments and shrines from the period which are still intact. Sonargaon is located outside of Dhaka. The Museum of Folk Art and Culture is located there.

SOUTH ASIAN ASSOCIATION FOR REGIONAL COOPERATION (SAARC). A regional group initiated by President Ziaur Rahman (q.v.). Member countries are Bangladesh, Bhutan, India, the Maldives, Nepal, Pakistan and Sri Lanka. Formally inaugurated at the first summit of the leaders of the seven nations at Dhaka in December 1985, the purpose is to have a forum for discussing regional and not bilateral issues. All decisions are to be on the basis of consensus rather than on majority principle.

SUHRAWARDY FAMILY. A family of great prominence in government and intellectual circles in Calcutta. Husain Shahid Suhrawardy (q.v.) was the son of Sir Zahid Suhrawardy, a judge of the Calcutta High Court. Another branch of the family, that of Maulana Obaidullah Suhrawardy (a great-uncle of Husain Shahid) included this important religious figure and his sons Mahmud, a member of the Council of State, and Sir Hasan, one-time vice-chancellor of Calcutta University. Sir Hasan's daughter, Shaista Suhrawardy Ikramullah, was a member of Parliament (her book From Purdah to Parliament describes the change in her life). Her husband, Ikramullah, was a foreign secretary of Pakistan (and his brother, Hidayatullah, a vice-president of India). Their daughter, Sarwath, is married to Crown Prince Hasan of Jordan. Through other connections, Husain Shahid Suhrawardy was related to Abul Hashim (q.v.), Sir Abdur Rahim (q.v.) (his daughter was Husain Shahid's first wife) and Fazlul Haq (q.v.).

SUHRAWARDY, HUSAIN SHAHID (1893-1963). Founder of the Awami League (q.v.) in 1949, had previously been a key member of the Muslim League (q.v.). He was a member of a prominent Bengali Muslim family (see Suhrawardy family) and was educated at Oxford and the Inns of Court in London. Having been a key elected official of the Calcutta municipality, he entered the Bengal Legislative Assembly in 1937 and served in the Fazlul Haq (q.v.) coalition cabinet (1937-1941) and in the Nazimuddin (q.v.) cabinet (1943-1945).

After the 1946 election, Suhrawardy successfully challenged Nazimuddin for the leadership of the Muslim League group in the assembly and became prime minister of Bengal, 1946-1947. The period was distinguished by the Great Calcutta Killing in August 1946, and then by Suhrawardy's working with Mahatma Gandhi to attempt (rather successfully) to tamp down the communal rioting. The period also saw Suhrawardy's floating of the concept of a third dominion to include Bengal and Assam as an eastern balance to Pakistan and "Hindustan." In this he had the support of some Congress party members, but incurred the wrath of Jinnah (q.v.).

Jinnah effectively barred Suhrawardy from continuing in office
as chief minister of East Bengal, a post to which Nazimuddin was
appointed.

In 1949, after a period of residence in India, Suhrawardy
floated his concept of a party which would include non-Muslims
as well as Muslims and founded the Awami League. This party,
which never gained significant strength in the western wing of
Pakistan, joined with the Krishak Sramik Party (q.v.) in the
United Front (q.v.) to defeat the Muslim League in the 1954
East Bengal legislature elections. Suhrawardy left the legislative leadership in East Bengal to Ataur Rahman Khan (q.v.) to
concentrate his attention on national politics. He was prime minister of Pakistan, 1956-1957. After martial law he opposed Ayub
Khan (q.v.) and worked for the restoration of the parliamentary
system. He died in Beirut on December 5, 1963.

SULTAN, MUHAMMAD (1928-1983). Founder-president of the East
   Pakistan Student Union, one of the most active student unions
   in the country. He joined the National Awami Party of Bhashani
   and was the secretary general of the party from 1966 to 1968.
   In 1970 he retired from politics and returned to his earlier profession in the book printing and publishing world. He always
   fought for Bengali nationalism and for that reason his books were
   banned. For his contribution to Bengali nationalism he was
   awarded the 21 February (see Martyrs' Day) award.

SWARNIRVAR. A district-level effort to boost agricultural production,
   began in 1974. Swarnirvar means "self-reliance." It was initially organized around a village committee on which all segments
   of the village would be represented. Some of the slogans of the
   swarnirvar movement were "Let the hands of beggars turn into
   the hands of workers" and "We will beg no more, we will not al-
   low the nation to beg."

SYLHET REFERENDUM. Held in 1947 in Sylhet District of Assam to
   determine whether that district would go to India or Pakistan in
   the partition. It was agreed that if the district voted for Pakistan the boundary commission would delimit the contiguous areas
   of Muslim majority. The district did vote to go to Pakistan. The
   subdivisions of Sylhet, Moulvi Bazar, Sunamganj and Habiganj
   were awarded to Pakistan with the subdivision of Karimganj
   going to India.

- T -

TAGORE, RABINDRANATH (SIR) (1861-1941). The most noted of
   modern Indian poets, winning the Nobel prize for literature in
   1912. His works are as well accepted by the Muslims of Bengal as they are by the Hindus. The banning of Tagore's works
   from Pakistan radio in 1965 by Khwaja Shahabuddin (q.v.) was

one of the straws which eventually broke the camel's back of
Pakistan's unity. One of Tagore's poems, Sonar Bangla (Golden
Bengal), serves as the national anthem of Bangladesh and an-
other of his poems is the national anthem of India.

TAMIZUDDIN KHAN (1889-1963). Active in the Congress, the Khilafat movement and the Muslim League (q.v.), achieving his official positions as a member of the League. He was a member of
the legislature in Bengal, 1926-46, and was elected to the Central
Legislative Assembly in 1946. He succeeded Jinnah (q.v.) as
president of the Pakistan Constituent Assembly in 1948 and held
the office until the assembly was dissolved by Governor General
Ghulam Muhammad (q.v.) in 1954.
    Tamizuddin challenged the dissolution in a notable case in
which, in effect, the judicial system stated that Tamizuddin was
correct in maintaining that the governor general had no right to
dissolve the assembly, but that the governor general had caused
a new assembly to be elected and, therefore, representative
government was restored. Tamizuddin returned to public office
as the speaker of the National Assembly elected in 1962, retaining that position until his death.

TARKABAGISH, MAULANA ABDUL RASHID (d. 1986). A prominent
member of the Muslim League (q.v.), left the Muslim League be-
cause of its policies in East Pakistan and joined the Awami
League (q.v.). He became the president of the East Pakistan
Awami League in 1957. He relinquished his position when Sheikh
Mujibur Rahman (q.v.) took over as the new leader. In 1976
he formed a new political party and named it the Gana Azad
League (People's Freedom League).

TIKKA KHAN (b. 1915). A military officer, was martial law administrator and governor of East Pakistan in 1971. In the latter
office, he succeeded Admiral S. M. Ahsan and was replaced later
in the year by A. M. Malik (q.v.). Described by Bangladeshis
as the "butcher of Bangladesh," he administered the province
during the worst period of the civil war. After retirement, he
entered politics in Pakistan as a member of the People's Party of
Pakistan, the group founded by Zulfiqar Ali Bhutto (q.v.).

TOAHA, MOHAMMAD (b. 1922). Associated with the communist movement in Bengal since the early 1950s. He was a member of the
Awami League (q.v.) and a close political associate of Sheikh
Mujibur Rahman (q.v.). He left the position of joint secretary
of the Awami League in 1957 and joined the National Awami Party
(q.v.) with Maulana Bhashani (q.v.). He was imprisoned in
1958 and released in 1967. He formed the Communist Party of
East Bengal in 1969 and went underground in 1972. Returning
to open politics in the late 1970s, he was elected to parliament
in 1979 as a member of the Samyabadi Dal--(Marxbadi, Leninbadi)
(Communist Party). He was the only communist member to be
elected.

TOFAZZUL HUSSAIN (1911-1969). Editor and proprietor of the newspaper Daily Ittefaq. He started his career as a civil servant but
resigned from the service in the late 1930s. His association with
H. S. Suhrawardy (q.v.) led him to be associated with the Muslim League (q.v.). In 1951 he established Ittefaq. He was a
renowned columnist and used his paper to express the desires
and expectations of the Bengali Muslims. His paper evolved into the mouthpiece of the Awami League (q.v.) which brought to-
gether leaders of Bengali nationalism. The newspaper was banned
and Tofazzul arrested during the Ayub (q.v.) regime. After
his death the Ittefaq group has been managed by his sons. The
paper did not support Mujibur Rahman's (q.v.) authoritarian
steps and was again proscribed. Ittefaq now has the largest
circulation of any daily in Bangladesh.

TRIBES. There are three distinct groups of tribals in Bangladesh.
One of these groups is comprised of tribes that are actually
southern extensions of tribes whose main bodies are in the states
of northeastern India. These include the Garos, Khasis and others residing in Mymensingh Region. The second group is located
primarily in the Chittagong Hill Tracts (q.v.) and the adjacent
Chittagong Region and is related to the peoples of Burma and
areas of India such as the state of Tripura. The largest of
these tribes are the Chakmas (48.1 percent of the tribal population of the Chittagong Hill Tracts), the Marmas (27.8 percent),
and the Tripuras (12.3 percent); none of the other nine groups
identified in the census comprises more than 4 percent of the
tribal population of the Chittagong Hill Tracts. It is from these
tribes that insurgency against the central government arises.
(See also Christianity and Buddhism.) One other tribal group,
the Santhals, originates from West Bengal and Orissa in India.
They are predominantly Hindu and are often employed in tea
estates.

TWENTY-ONE POINTS. The election manifesto of the United Front
(q.v.), was used during the East Pakistan provincial election of
1954. Among the twenty-one points were: the recognition of
Bengali as an official language of Pakistan; complete autonomy
for East Bengal in all matters except defense, foreign affairs
and currency; headquarters of the navy be located in East Bengal; land reform be instituted and surplus land be given to the
landless; irrigation be improved; agricultural cooperatives be
set up; agricultural production be increased; jute trade be nationalized; discrimination against Bengalis in the armed forces
cease; the repeal of laws which allowed imprisonment without
trial; and labor conventions of the International Labor Organization be practiced.

- U -

UNION OF SOVIET SOCIALIST REPUBLICS. Initially, relations

between Bangladesh and the Soviet Union were cordial, in recognition of Soviet support for Bangladeshi independence. Some members of the cabinet of Mujibur Rahman (q.v.), such as Tajuddin Ahmad (q.v.), were reported to have favored a treaty of friendship with the Soviet Union along the lines of the Indo-Soviet treaty of 1971.

The Soviets gave assistance to the rehabilitation of Bangladesh, especially the clearing of Chittagong Harbor. However, after the death of Mujib, the large Soviet presence became suspect in the eyes of the new leadership. Bangladesh strongly opposed the 1979 Soviet invasion of Afghanistan and Soviet support to Vietnam's actions in Kampuchea. In 1983-84, the Ershad regime ousted a number of Soviet diplomats and officials on the grounds that they were acting against Bangladesh. Relations since have been correct if not cordial. The Soviet Union supplied limited military assistance during the Mujib period and continues to give limited economic aid. It also sponsors a substantial number of scholarships for study in the Soviet Union.

UNITED FRONT (UF). An umbrella political grouping consisting of the Awami League (q.v.), the Krishak Sramik Party (q.v.), the Nizam-i-Islam (q.v.), Ganotantrik Dal (q.v.) and some smaller political parties. It was formed to oppose the Pakistan Muslim League in the East Pakistan provincial election of 1954. A twenty-one point manifesto (q.v.) which centered around the importance of the Bengali language, regional autonomy, limitations of the powers of the central government and rejection of the Basic Principles Committee (q.v.) report won for the UF strong public support. The UF won an overwhelming victory and formed the first non-Muslim League government in April 1954. The East Pakistan Legislative Assembly had a total of 309 seats of which the UF won 237 and Muslim League won only 10. In May 1954 the UF government was dismissed by the central government because of the purportedly anti-Pakistani statements of the UF leaders.

UNITED NATIONS. Bangladesh became a member of the United Nations in 1974, following the withdrawal of the veto by China (q.v.) that had been exercised at the request of Pakistan (q.v.). Bangladesh was elected to the Security Council in 1978, winning election against Japan for the "Asian seat." In 1986, Bangladeshi Foreign Minister Humayun Rashid Choudhury was elected president of the General Assembly. Bangladesh is also a member of the affiliated agencies of the United Nations. It was chairman of the Group of 77 in 1982-1983 (see Foreign Policy).

UNITED STATES. Relations with the United States were difficult, initially, as the result of the American "tilt" toward Pakistan in the civil war. The United States delayed formal recognition of the new state until February 1972. However, American assistance for rehabilitation had already begun to flow from the United States

government and from a wide range of private organizations.
Bangladesh also recalled the nearly unanimous support for it
from American academics and social organizations and from much
of the press and many in Congress. Despite some opposition
from some members of his cabinet (see Tajuddin Ahmad), Mujibur
Rahman (q.v.) saw the United States as the major source of the
assistance he badly needed. He also visited the United States.
Relations from the latter part of the Mujib period through the
regimes of his successors have developed a high degree of cordi-
ality and cooperation.

The United States is the largest donor of economic assistance
in the period since 1971, although in some recent years the commitments of Japan have exceeded those of the United States
among national donors (in some years commitments by international financial organizations, such as the International Development Association, have been higher than bilateral arrangements).
The United States has refused to give military assistance to
Bangladesh other than a modest grant for training. American
activity in educational programs has been much less than that of
the Soviet Union (see Union of Soviet Socialist Republics).

- V -

VANGA.   The name used in ancient Hindu literature for Bengal.
The Sanskritic "v" is changed in Bengali to a "b."

VERNACULAR ELITE.   A term applied to the Bengali Muslim leadership which used Bengali as a family and political language, as
opposed to the national elite (q.v.) which used Urdu.   Most
prominent of this group both before and after Pakistani independence was Fazlul Haq (q.v.).   He used Bengali to appeal to
the masses and formed the Krishak Praja Party (q.v.) to represent their interests.   He and others in the group were concerned with the matters of Bengal first and of Muslims elsewhere
in India second.   After independence, Fazlul Haq was joined by
Suhrawardy (q.v.) whose Awami League (q.v.) was almost entirely an East Bengal party.   Mujibur Rahman (q.v.) represented the group most prominently in the later years of the rule
of Ayub Khan (q.v.) and in the first period of Bangladeshi independence.

- W -

WAHIDUZZAMAN (1912-1976).   A successful businessman, entered
politics as an associate of A. K. Fazlul Haq (q.v.) and was
elected to the Bengal Legislative Assembly in 1942.   After Pakistani independence, however, he joined the Muslim League and
was a member of the constituent assembly, 1951-1955.   During
the rule of Ayub Khan (q.v.) he was minister of commerce,

1962-1965. He left the Muslim League in 1969 and supported the movement against Ayub for the restoration of democracy.

WOMEN. Women play a mixed role in Bangladesh. The rate of women's literacy, for example, is much lower than that of men, 13 percent compared to 26 percent (1981). In rural areas, women are members of the family farming team and are expected to perform chores assigned to them as well as household work and the rearing of children. In urban areas, most women who are employed are in menial and often physically taxing jobs such as construction. Despite this, at the higher educational levels, opportunities for women may be greater than in most Muslim countries. There are a fair number of women doctors, lawyers and teachers in higher education and performing similar roles. The leaders of the two principal groups opposing Ershad (q.v.) are women: Sheikh Hasina Wajid (q.v.) of the Awami League (q.v.) and Khalida Zia (see Ziaur Rahman) of the Bangladesh Nationalist Party (q.v.). (See also Education, Health Delivery and Population Planning.)

- Y -

YAHYA KHAN, AGHA MUHAMMAD (1917-1980). A career military officer, was president of Pakistan, 1969-1971, succeeding Ayub Khan (q.v.). He entered the British Indian army in 1938. He was commander in East Pakistan from 1962 until 1966 when he became deputy commander-in-chief of the army. From that position, he replaced Ayub as president in March 1969, in a palace coup. With the loss by the Pakistan army to the Mukti Bahini (q.v.) and their Indian allies in December 1971, Yahya resigned the presidency and turned the government over to Zulfiqar Ali Bhutto (q.v.).

- Z -

ZAHIR RAIHAN (1933-1971). Jailed for his participation in the movement to make Bengali one of the national languages of Pakistan. He began his career as a movie director in 1956 and is most famous for his documentary Stop Genocide which showed the atrocities committed by the Pakistani army in Bangladesh. He was killed by the Pakistani army and was given a posthumous Bangla Academy award. He was a nationalist and his movies all carried this theme.

ZAHURUL HUQUE (1935-1969). One of the co-accused in the Agartala conspiracy case against Sheikh Mujibur Rahman (q.v.). In what was described as an attempt to escape, he was shot dead by the Pakistan army.

ZAINUL ABEDIN (d. 1976). A National Professor of the Arts, a title bestowed on him by Sheikh Mujibur Rahman (q.v.). He is most famous for his more than 100 black-and-white sketches of the Calcutta famine of 1943. He is also well known for his abstract painting.

ZIAUR RAHMAN (1936-1981). The effective leader of Bangladesh from 1975 to 1981. An army officer commissioned in 1953, he rose to the rank of major in 1971. In the civil war, he led his unit against the Pakistani army and proclaimed Bangladeshi independence on March 27, 1971, with himself as provisional president. This act apparently earned him the displeasure of Mujibur Rahman (q.v.) under whose regime Zia's career did not prosper to the extent that other Mukti Bahini (q.v.) leaders' careers did. Following the assassination of Mujib, Zia was appointed chief of staff of the army in August 1975. Although displaced briefly during the coup attempt by Khalid Musharif (q.v.), Zia emerged from the November 1975 coups as the dominant leader of the country. He was designated deputy chief martial law administrator then and replaced President A. S. M. Sayem (q.v.) as chief martial law administrator in 1976.

With Sayem's retirement from the presidency for purported health reasons, Zia became president in 1977. He had this confirmed through a referendum, but then won the post in a contested election in 1978, defeating M. A. G. Osmany (q.v.) and others. Zia remained president until his assassination on May 30, 1981. Not considered a likely candidate for a charismatic role, he nonetheless created one for himself and provided capable and pragmatic leadership emphasizing such points as rural development, food self-sufficiency and family planning. He is also regarded as the "father" of the South Asian Association for Regional Cooperation (q.v.).

BIBLIOGRAPHY

GENERAL WORKS

REFERENCE, INFORMATION, GENERAL HISTORY

Ali, Syed Murtaza. History of Chittagong. Dacca: Standard Publishers, 1964.

American University, Washington, DC, Foreign Area Studies. Area Handbook for Bangladesh. Washington, DC: U.S. Government Printing Office, 1975.

Bangladesh Ministry of Information and Broadcasting. Bangladesh Progress: 1974. Dacca: Department of Publications, Ministry of Information and Broadcasting, 1975.

Chen, Lincoln C. Disaster in Bangladesh. London: Oxford University Press, 1973.

Hashyap, Subhash C. Bangla Desh: Backgrounds and Perspectives. New York: International Publications Services, 1972.

Hossain, Anwar. The Bangladesh Image. Dhaka, Bangladesh: Padma Printers, 1980.

Johnson, Basil Leonard Clyde. Bangladesh. 2nd ed. London: Heinemann Educational Books; New York: Barnes and Noble Books, 1982.

Kashyap, S. C. Bangla Desh, Background and Perspectives. New Delhi: Institute of Constitutional and Parliamentary Studies, 1971.

Malik, Amita. The Year of the Vulture. New Delhi, India: Orient Longman, 1972.

Marek, Jan. Bangladesh lidova republika. Praha: Nakl. Svoboda, 1980.

Mascarenhas, Anthony. The Rape of Bangla Desh. Delhi: Vikas Publications, 1971.

Naruzzaman, M. Who's Who. Dacca: Hasana Hena, 1986.

Nicholas, Marta, and Philip Oldenburg. Bangladesh, The Birth of a Nation: A Handbook of Background Information and Documentary Sources. Madras: M. Seshachalam, 1972.

Pavithran, A. K. Bangladesh: Principles and Perspectives. Calcutta: W. W. Grant, 1971.

Quaderi, F. Quader. Bangladesh Genocide and World Press. Dacca: Quaderi, 1972.

Rahman, Choudhury Shamsur. Bangladesh: Land and People. Dacca: Department of Publications, Ministry of Information and Broadcasting, 1973.

Rahman, M. Bangladesh Today: An Indictment and a Lament. London: News and Media Ltd., 1978.

Sharif, Ahmed. Dacca, Pakistan. Dacca, Bangladesh: Asiatic Society of Bangladesh, 1965.

Singh, Sheelendra, ed. Bangladesh Documents. New York: International Publications Service, 1973.

U.S. Library of Congress, American Libraries Book Procurement Center, New Delhi. Accessions List, Bangladesh 1972. New Delhi: 1972.

TRAVEL AND DESCRIPTION

Chatterjee, Basant Kumar. Inside Bangladesh Today, An Eye-
Witness Account. New Delhi: S. Chand, 1973.

Indian International Trade Centre. Business Guide to Bangladesh.
Bombay: 1972.

Mahajan, Jagmohan. The Ganga Trail, Foreign Accounts and Sketches
of the River Scene. New Delhi: Clarion Books, 1984.

Mahmood, Abu Zafar Shahabuddin. Introducing East Pakistan, Geography, Everyday Life, Places of Interest. Dacca: Roushan
Akhter Begum, 1969.

Yeo, Don. Bangladesh: A Traveller's Guide. London: Roger
Lascelles, 1984.

BIBLIOGRAPHY

Bangladesh Forms and Publications Office. Catalogue of Publications.
Dacca: Forms and Publications Office, 1973.

Begum, N. Nur. Social and Administrative Research in Bangladesh:
An Annotated Bibliography. Dacca: National Institute of
Public Administration, 1973.

Haque, Serajul. Bangladesh Demography: A Select Bibliography.
Dacca: Bangladesh Institute of Development Studies, 1976.

Ministry of External Affairs, New Delhi. Bangladesh Documents.
Madras: B. N. K. Press Private Limited, 1971.

Patterson, Maureen L. P. South Asian Civilizations: A Bibliographic
Synthesis. Chicago: University of Chicago Press, 1981.

Satyaprakash. Bangladesh, A Select Bibliography. New Delhi: Indian Documentation Service, 1976.

Serajul Haque. Bangladesh Demography: A Select Bibliography. Dacca: Bangladesh Institute of Development Studies, 1976.

Shamsuddoulah, A. B. M. Introducing Bangladesh Through Books, A Select Bibliography, With Introduction and Annotations 1855-1976. Dacca: Great Eastern Books, 1976.

Talukdar, Alauddin. Bangladesh Economy: A Select Bibliography. Dacca: Bangladesh Institute of Development Studies, 1976.

_____. Bangladesh Industry Studies: A Select Bibliography. Dacca: Bangladesh Institute of Development Studies, 1975.

AUDIOVISUAL INFORMATION

Bangladesh. Color Film, 16mm, 8 min. Contemporary Films.

Bangladesh: A Beginning or an End? Color Film, 16mm, 15 min. Department of State.

Bangladesh: A Nation's Search for Identity. Color Film, 16 mm, 50 min. Producer: not available.

Haq, Enamul. Meet Bangladesh. Dacca: Department of Films and Publications, Government of Bangladesh, 1979.

Kabir, Alamgir. Film in Bangladesh. Dacca: Bangla Academy, 1979.

CULTURAL

ARCHITECTURE AND ARTS

Bangladesh: Inter-Cultural Studies. Marshall W. Fishwick (ed.). Dhaka: n.p., 1983.

Dacca, Women for Women Research and Study Group. Women for Women: Bangladesh 1975. Dacca: The Women's Research and Study Group, 1975.

Haider, Azimusshan. Dacca: History and Romance in Place Names; An Analytical Account of the Nomenclature of Roads and Localities in Dacca with a Discussion of the Rationale for Their Retention or Otherwise. Dacca: Dacca Municipality, 1967.

Hasan, Sayed Mahmudul. Sonargaon. Dhaka: Bangladesh Folk Art and Crafts Foundation, 1982.

_____. Dacca, Gateway to the East. Dacca: Research Centre for Islamic Art and Culture, 1982.

Islam, A. K. M. Aminul. A Bangladesh Village: Conflict and Cohesion. Cambridge, MA: Schenkman, 1974.

Jahangir, Burhanuddin Khan. Contemporary Painters: Bangladesh. Dacca: Bengali Academy, 1974.

Karim, Abdul. Dacca: The Mughal Capital. Dacca: Asiatic Society of Bangladesh, 1964.

Morrison, Barrie M. Lalmai. A Cultural Center of Early Bengal: An Archaeological Report and Historical Analysis. Seattle: University of Washington Press, 1974.

BENGALI LANGUAGE, LITERATURE, AND LINGUISTICS

Ashraf, Sayed Ali. Muslim Traditions in Bengali Literature. Karachi: Bengal Literature Society, University of Karachi, 1960.

Bangla Desh: A Voice of a New Nation. Pritish Nandy (Trans.). Calcutta: Dialogue Publications, 1971.

Chowdhury, Kabir, ed. Folk Tales of Bangladesh. Dacca: Bengali Academy, 1972.

Currimbhoy, Asif. Sonar Bangla: A Play in Four Acts. Calcutta: Writers' Workshop, 1972.

Halder, Gopal. Kazi Nazrul Islam. New Delhi: Sahitya Akademi, 1973.

Haq, Muhammad Enamul. Muslim Bengali Literature. Karachi: Pakistan Publications, 1957.

Haq, Shamsul. Bengali Literature, A Bibliography 1947-1969. Dacca: Jatiya Granthakendra, 1970.

Jasimuddin. Folk Tales of Bangladesh. Dacca: Oxford University Press, 1974.

Kripalani, Krishna. Rabindranath Tagore: A Biography. New York: Oxford University Press, 1962.

Laure, Jason and Ettagale Laure. Joi Bangla: The Children of Bangladesh. FS&G, 1974.

Siddiqui, Ashraf. Folkloric Bangladesh: A Collection of Essays on Folk Literature of Bangladesh. Dacca: Bangla Academy, 1976.

Walsh, Jay, and Patricia C. Oviatt. Ripe Mangoes: Miracle Missionary Stories from Bangladesh. N.p.: Reg Baptist, 1978.

SCIENCE

GEOGRAPHY

Rashid, Haroun Er. Geography of Bangladesh. Boulder, Colorado: Westview Press, 1978.

Stoeckel, J., and Moqbul A. Choudhury. Fertility, Infant Mortality and Family Planning in Rural Bangladesh. Dacca: Oxford University Press, 1973.

U.S. Board on Geography Names. Bangladesh. Washington: U.S. Government Printing Office, 1976.

SOCIOLOGY

ANTHROPOLOGY

Barket, Khuda E. Power Structure in Rural Bangladesh: Some
Reflections from a Village in Commilla. Canberra: Australian
National University Press, 1981.

Hartman, Betsy, and James K. Boyce. A Quiet Violence: View from
a Bangladesh Village. London: Zed Press, 1983.

_____. Needless Hunger: Voices from a Bangladesh Village.
San Francisco, CA: Institute for Food and Development Policy,
1979.

DEMOGRAPHY AND POPULATION

Bangladesh Census of Population 1974: Provisional Results. Dacca:
Census Commission, Ministry of Home Affairs, Govt. of the
People's Republic of Bangladesh, 1974.

Bangladesh Fertility Survey 1975: A Summary of Findings. The
Hague: International Statistical Institute, 1979.

Bangladesh Fertility Survey 1975-76: Report. Dacca: Ministry of
Health and Population Control, Population Control and Family
Planning Division, Govt. of the People's Republic of Bangla-
desh, 1978- .

Bangladesh National Population Policy: An Outline. Dacca: Government of the People's Republic of Bangladesh, Population Control and Family Planning Divsiion, 1976.

Green, Lawrence W. The Dacca Family Planning Experiment: A
Comparative Evaluation of Programs Directed at Males and at
Females. Berkeley: University of California, School of Public
Health, 1972.

Khan, Mashiur Rahman. Bangladesh Population During the First Five-
Year Plan Period, 1972-77 ... etc. Dacca: Bangladesh Institute of Development Studies, 1972.

National Research Council Committee on Population and Demography. Estimation of Recent Trends in Fertility and Mortality in Bangladesh. Washington, DC: National Academy of Sciences, 1981.

SOCIETY AND SOCIAL CONDITION

Abdullah, T., and S. Zeidenstein. Village Women of Bangladesh: Prospects for Change. New York: Pergamon Press, 1981.

Alamgir, Mohiuddin. Famine in South Asia, Political Economy of Mass Starvation. Cambridge, MA: Oelgeschlager, Gunn & Hain, 1980.

Arens, J., and J. V. Bewden. Jhagrapur: Poor Peasants and Women in a Village in Bangladesh. Birmingham, England: Third World Publications, 1977.

Chatterji, Tapan Mohan. Alpona: Ritual Decoration in Bengal. Bombay: Orient Longmans, 1948.

Chowdhury, Anwarullah. A Bangladesh Village: A Study in Social Stratification. Dacca: Centre for Social Studies, 1978.

Dacca, Women for Women Research and Study Group. Women for Women: Bangladesh 1975. Dacca: The Women's Research and Study Group, 1975.

Hafeez, Zaidi S. M. The Village Culture in Transition: A Study of East Pakistan Rural Society. Honolulu: East-West Center, 1971.

Islam, A. K. M. Aminul. A Bangladesh Village: Conflict and Cohesion. Cambridge, MA: Schenkman, 1974.

Khan, A. M. Majeed. Experience in Cross Cultural Living. Comilla: Bangladesh Academy for Rural Development, 1964.

Mukherjee, Ramkrishna. Six Villages of Bengal. Bombay: Popular Prakashan, 1971.

Rahman, Atiur. The Crisis of External Dependence: The Political
Economy of Foreign Aid to Bangladesh. London: Zed, 1982.

Sattar, Abdus. Tribal Culture in Bangladesh. Dacca: Muktadhara,
1974.

Schendel, Willem van. Pleasant Mobility, the Odds of Life in Rural
Bangladesh. Assen, Netherlands: Van Gorcum, 1981.

RELIGION

Anwarul Karim, Abu Sayeed Mohammad. The Bauls of Bangladesh:
A Study of an Obscure Religious Cult. Kushtia: Lalan Academy, 1980.

Banerjee, Sanat Kumar. Bangladesh Hindus: Agonised Quest for
Cultural Emancipation. Calcutta: Swastik Prakashan Trust,
1978.

Chakravarti, Surath Chandra. Bauls, The Spiritual Vikings. Calcutta: Firma KLM, 1980.

Chatterjee, Rama. Religion in Bengal. Calcutta: Punthi Pustak,
1985.

EDUCATION

Bangladesh Education Directorate. Education in Bangladesh. Dacca:
Bangladesh Government Press, 1974.

Haider, Muhiuddin. Village Level Integrated Population Education:
A Case Study of Bangladesh. Lanham, MD: University
Press of America, 1982.

Integrated Rural Development and the Role of Education. Report of
the Bangladesh/UNESCO Field Operational Seminar held in
Bangladesh March 1979. Paris: UNESCO, 1980.

Islam, Taherul. Social Justice and Education System in Bangladesh.
Dacca: Bureau of Economic Research, Dacca University, 1974.

Pakistan, East Bengal, Educational System Reconstruction Committee. Report of the East Bengal Educational System Reconstruction Committee. Dacca: Pakistan Government Press, 1952.

Puttick, Edwin B., et al. The Finance of Non Government Schools in Bangladesh. Berkeley: School of Education, University of California, 1974.

HISTORY

EARLY HISTORY

Ahmed, Sufia. Muslim Community in Bengal, 1884-1912. Dacca: Oxford University Press, 1974.

Bhattacharjee, Arun. Dateline Bangladesh. Bombay: Jaico Publishing House, 1971.

Broomfield, John. Elite Conflict in a Plural Society: Twentieth-Century Bengal. Berkeley: University of California Press, 1984.

Gopal, Ram. How the British Occupied Bengal. Calcutta: Asia Publishing House, 1963.

Gordon, Leonard A. Bengal: The Nationalist Movement 1876-1940. New York: Columbia University Press, 1974.

Grant, Colesworth. Rural Life in Bengal. Calcutta: W. Thacker & Co., 1859.

Hunter, William Wilson. Annals of Rural Bengal. New York: Johnson Reprint Corporation, 1970.

Inden, Ronald B. Marriage Rank in Bengali Culture. Berkeley: University of California Press, 1976.

Karim, Abdul. Corpus of the Muslim Coins of Bengal. Dacca: The Asiatic Society of Pakistan, 1960.

_____. Murshid Quli Khan and His Times. Dacca: The Asiatic Society of Pakistan, 1963.

_____. Social History of the Muslims in Bengal. Dacca: The Asiatic Society of Pakistan, 1959.

Khan, Abdul Majed. The Transition in Bengal 1765-1775. Cambridge, England: Cambridge University Press, 1969.

Khan, Muin-Ud-Din Ahmad. History of the Fara'idi Movement in Bengal 1818-1906. Karachi: 1965.

Kopf, David. British Orientalism and the Bengal Renaissance. Berkeley: University of California Press, 1969.

Mahmood, A. Z. Shehabuddin. Introducing East Pakistan. Dacca: Roushan Ara Begum Publishers, 1969.

Majumdar, R. C., and Jadunath Sarkar. (Eds.) The History of Bengal. University of Dhaka, 2 vols., 1942 and 1948.

Mallick, Azizur Rahman. British Policy and the Muslim in Bengal 1757-1856. Dacca: Asiatic Society of Pakistan, 1961.

Ray, Rajat Kanta. Social Conflict and Political Unrest in Bengal 1875-1927. Calcutta: Oxford University Press, 1984.

Reid, Robert. Years of Change in Bengal. London: Ernest Benn. Ltd., 1966.

Sarkar, Jadunath (ed.). The History of Bengal: Muslim Period 1200-1757. Patna, India: Academica Asiatica, 1973.

Sarkar, Sumit. The Swadeshi Movement in Bengal 1903-1908. New Delhi: n.p., 1973.

Sinha, Narendra Krishna (ed.). The History of Bengal (1757-1905). University of Calcutta, 1967.

Tarafdar, Momtazur Rahman [and Husain Shahi?]. Bengal. Dacca: Asiatic Society of Pakistan, 1965.

MODERN HISTORY

Ahmad, Kamruddin. The Social History of East Pakistan. Dacca: Mrs. Raushan Ara Ahmed Publisher, 1967.

Bertocci, Peter, ed. Bangladesh, History, Society and Culture. East Lansing: Asian Studies Center, Michigan State University, 1973.

Bhattacharjee, G. P. Renaissance and Freedom Movement in Bangladesh. Calcutta: The Minerva Associates, 1973.

Chakravarty, S. R. Bangladesh. Virendra Narain. New Delhi: South Asian Publishers, 1986.

Ermoshkin, Nikolai Ivanovich. Bangladesh--gody bor'by i stanovleniia. Moskva: Nauka, 1979.

Franda, Marcus. Bangladesh: The First Decade. New Delhi: South Asia Publishers, 1982.

Gill, Stephen M. Discovery of Bangladesh. New York: n.p., 1975.

Hasanat, Abul. Bangladesh, Sufferings, Surfacing, Survival: Let Humanity Not Forget the Ugliest Genocide. Dacca: Muktadhara, 1978.

Islam, A. K. M. Aminul. Victorious Victims, Political Transformation in a Traditional Society. Cambridge, MA: Schenkman, 1978.

Kashyap, B. Bangladesh: Background and Perspectives. New Delhi: National Publishing House, 1971.

Kayastha, Ved P. The Crisis in the Indian Subcontinent and the Birth of Bangladesh. Ithaca, NY: Cornell University Press, 1972.

Keesing's Contemporary Archives. Pakistan: From 1947 to the Creation of Bangladesh. New York: Scribner, 1973.

Mascarenhas, Anthony. Bangladesh: A Legacy of Blood. London: Hodder and Stoughton, 1986.

O'Donnell, Charles Peter. Bangladesh, Biography of a Muslim Nation. Boulder, CO: Westview, 1984.

Payne, Robert. Massacre. New York: Macmillan, 1973.

Sen Gupta, Jyoti. History of Freedom Movement in Bangladesh. Columbia, MO: South Asia Books, 1974.

Singh, Mala. (Ed.) Khushwant Singh on War and Peace in India, Pakistan and Bangladesh. Delhi: n. pub., 1976.

Thapar, Romila. From Lineage to State, Social Formations in the Mid-first Millennium B.C. in the Ganga Valley.. Bombay: Oxford University Press, 1984.

Thomas, Barbara, and Spencer Lavan. West Bengal and Bangladesh: Perspectives from 1972. East Lansing, MI: Michigan State University, 1972.

POLITICS

GOVERNMENT, ADMINISTRATION AND POLITICS

Abedin, Najmul. Local Administration and Politics in Modernising Societies: Bangladesh and Pakistan. Dacca: National Institute of Public Administration, 1974.

Ahmad, Kabir Uddin. Break-up of Pakistan: Background and Prospects of Bangladesh. London: Social Science Pub., 1975.

Ahmed, Iftikhar. Technological Change and Agrarian Structure: A Study of Bangladesh. Geneva: International Labour Office, 1981.

Ali, S. M. After the Dark Night. Problems of Sheikh Mujibur Rahman. Delhi: Vikas, 1973.

Ali, Shaikh Magsood, et al. Decentralization and People's Participation in Bangladesh. Dacca: National Institute of Public Administration, 1983.

Allen, B. C. Eastern Bengal District Gazetteer. Dacca: Allahabad, The Pioneer Press, 1912.

Anisuzzaman, M. Bangladesh Public Administration and Society. Dacca: Bangladesh Books International Limited, 1979.

Ayoob, Mohammed (and others). Bangladesh, A Struggle for Nationhood. Delhi: Vikas Publications, 1971.

Bangladesh; A Souvenir on the First Anniversary of Victory Day, December 16, 1972. [Board of eds: Syed Ali Ahsan, Ch., and others.] Dacca: Ministry of Information and Broadcasting, Govt. of the People's Republic of Bangladesh, 1972.

The Bangladesh Code. Dacca: Ministry of Law and Parliamentary Affairs, Govt. of the People's Republic of Bangladesh, 1987.

Bangladesh Customs, Excise, and Sales Tax Tariff. 2nd ed., corrected up to 1st March 1976. Dhaka: The Ministry of Finance and Planning, National Board of Revenue, Govt. of the People's Republic of Bangladesh, 1976.

Bangladesh Customs, Excise, and Sales Tax Tariff. 3rd ed., Dhaka: The Ministry of Finance and Planning, National Board of Revenue, Govt. of the People's Republic of Bangladesh, 1983.

Bangladesh Labour Code: As Modified Up-to-date. A. A. Khan (ed.). Dhaka: Khoshroz Kitab Mahal, 1985.

Bangladesh Legal Practitioners and Bar Council Order, 1972. Dacca: Bangladesh Bar Council, 1980.

Bangladesh, Ministry of Law, Parliamentary Affairs and Justice. The

Constitution of the People's Republic of Bangladesh. Dacca: Bangladesh Forms and Publications Office, 1975.

The Bangladesh Registration Manual, 1983. Dhaka: Deputy Controller, Govt. Print. Press, 1984.

Bangladesh, Society, Politics and Bureaucracy. Mohammad Mohabbat Khan and John P. Thorp (eds.). Dhaka: Center for Administrative Studies, 1984.

Bangladesh Speaks. Dacca: Bangladesh Government Printing Office, 1972.

Bangladesh Standard Trade Classification (BSTC), July 1980. Dacca: Bureau of Statistics, Ministry of Planning, Govt. of the People's Republic of Bangladesh, 1980.

Bangladesh Studies: Politics, Administration, Rural Development and Foreign Policy. Mohammad Mohabbat Khan and Syed Anwar Husain (eds.). Dhaka: n.pub., n.d.

Barua, Tushar Kanti. Political Elite in Bangladesh: A Socio-Anthropological and Historical Analysis of the Processes of Their Formation. Bern: P. Lang, 1978.

Baxter, Craig. Bangladesh: A New Nation in an Old Setting. Boulder: Westview Press, 1984.

Bhuiyan, Abdul W. Emergence of Bangladesh and the Rule of the Awami League. Advent, NY: Vikas India, 1982.

Blair, Harry W. The Elusiveness of Equity: Institutional Approaches to Rural Development in Bangladesh. Ithaca, NY: Rural Development Committee, Center for International Studies, Cornell University, 1974.

Chatterjee, Basant. Inside Bangladesh Today. New Delhi: S. Chand & Co., 1973.

Chaudhuri, Kalyan. Genocide in Bangladesh. Kennikat, n.p.: n.p., 1972.

Chopra, Pran. The Challenge of Bangladesh. Bombay: Humanities Press, 1971.

Chowdhury, Subrata Roy. The Genesis of Bangladesh. New York: Asia Publishing House, 1972.

Dimov, Khristo. Bangladesh--trudniiat put na edin narod. Sofiia: Partizdat, 1980.

Franda, Marcus. Bangladesh: The First Decade. Hanover, NH: Universities Field Staff International. New Delhi: South Asian Publishers, 1981.

Franda, Marcus. Bangladesh Nationalism and Ziaur Rahman's Presidency. Hanover, NH: American Universities Field Staff, 1981.

Friis, Henning Kristian. Bangladesh Social Science Research Council: Its Objectives, Functions, and Organisation. Dacca: Ford Foundation, 1974.

Ghani, Osman, and Mozammel Haque. The Bangladesh Penal Code. Dacca: Khoshroz Kitab Mahal, 1974.

Jahan, Rounaq. Bangladesh Politics: Problems and Issues. Dacca: Dacca University Press, 1980.

Kabir, Mohammad G. Minority Politics in Bangladesh. New Delhi: Vikas, 1980.

Kamal, K. A. Sheikh Mujibur Rahman And Birth of Bangladesh. Dhaka: K. G. Ahmed, 1972.

Karim, A. Nazmul. The Dynamics of Bangladesh Society. Delhi: Vikas, 1980.

Khan, Mohammad M., and John P. Thorp. Bangladesh: Society, Politics and Bureaucracy. Riverdale, MD: Riverdale Co., 1985.

Khan, Mohammad Mohabbat, and Habib Mohammad Zafarullah. Politics and Bureaucracy in a New Nation Bangladesh. Dacca: Center for Administrative Studies, 1980.

Khan, Zillur R. Leadership in the Least Developed Nation: Bangladesh. Syracuse U. Foreign Comp., 1983.

Kurland, Gerald. The Creation of Bangla Desh. Sam Har Printers, 1973.

Lifschultz, Larry. Bangladesh: The Unfinished Revolution. London: Zed Press, 1979.

Lyon, Peter. Bangladesh Since Mujib. John Eppstein (ed.). London: Atlantic Education Trust, 1976.

Maniruzzaman, Talukdar. Radical Politics and the Emergency of Bangladesh. Dacca: Bangladesh Books International Limited, 1975.

_____. Bangladesh Revolution and Its Aftermath. New Delhi: South Asia Books, 1981.

_____. Group Interests and Political Changes: Studies of Pakistan and Bangladesh. New Delhi: South Asia Books, 1982.

Momen, Nurul. Bangladesh, The First Four Years (from 16 December 1971 to 15 December 1975). Dacca: Bangladesh Institute of Law & International Affairs, 1980.

Muhith, Abul Maal Abdul. Bangladesh: The Emergence of a Nation. Dhaka: Bangladesh Book International, 1978.

Munim, F. K. M. Rights of the Citizens Under the Constitution and Law. Dacca: Bangladesh Institute of Law and International Affairs, 1975.

Olsen, Viggo, and Jeanette Lokerbie. Daktar: Diplomat in Bangladesh. Chicago: Moody Press, 1973.

Rahman, Mizanur. Emergence of a New Nation in a Multi-Polar World: Bangladesh. Washington, DC: University Press of America, 1978.

Rahman, Sheikh Mujibur. Bangladesh, My Bangladesh: Selected Speeches and Statements October 28, 1970 to March 26, 1971. Delhi: Orient Longmans, 1972.

Rashiduzzaman, M. Rural Leadership and Population Control in Bangladesh. Washington, DC: University Press of America, 1982.

Razzaq, Abdur. Bangladesh, State of the Nation. Dacca: University of Dacca, 1981.

Sen Gupta, Jyoti. Bangladesh, In Blood and Tears. Calcutta: Naya Prokash, 1981.

Shiv Lal. Bangla-Pak Polities. New Delhi: Election Archives, 1985.

Umar, Badruddin. Politics and Society in East Pakistan and Bangladesh. Dacca: Mowla Brothers, 1973.

INTERNATIONAL RELATIONS

Ayoob, M. India, Pakistan, and Bangladesh: Search for a New Relationship. New Delhi: Vikas, 1975.

Bangladesh and UNCTAD V. K. M. Matin (ed.). Dacca: Bangladesh Institute of Development Studies, 1982.

Bangladesh: Reminiscences and the New Tragedy. Assam Province, India: United Publishers, 197- .

Beglova, N. S. Bangladesh, Iuzhnaia Aziia I Politika SShA. Moskva: Izd-vo "Nauka," 1982.

Brown, W. Norman. The United States and India, Pakistan and Bangladesh. Cambridge: Harvard University Press, 1972.

Choudhury, G. W. India, Pakistan, Bangladesh and the Major Powers. New York: The Free Press, 1975.

Faaland, Just. Aid and Influence: The Case of Bangladesh. New York: St. Martin's, 1980.

Franda, Marcus F. Bangladesh and India: Politics, Population, & Resources in a Global Environment. Hanover, NH: American Universities Field Staff, 1976.

Gandhi, Indira. India and Bangladesh: Selected Speeches and Statements March to December 1971. New Delhi: Orient Long- mans, 1972.

Ghosh, Sucheta. The Role of India in the Emergence of Bangladesh. New Delhi: South Asia Books, 1984.

Gustafson, W. Eric, ed. Pakistan and Bangladesh. Islamabad, Pak- istan: University of Islamabad Press, 1976.

Haque, Mahmudul. Bangladesh and Non-Alignment, 1971-75. Dacca: Forum for International Affairs, 1978.

International Journal. India, Pakistan, Bangladesh. Toronto: Canadian Institute of International Affairs, 1972.

Jackson, Robert. South Asian Crisis, Indian-Pakistan-Bangladesh. London: Chatto and Windus, 1975.

Jain, J. D. China, Pakistan and Bangladesh. New Delhi: Radiant Publishers, 1974.

Khan, Saadullah. East Pakistan to Bangladesh. Columbia, MO: South Asia Books, 1975.

Ministry of Foreign Affairs. SARC Documents. Dhaka: Eastern Commercial Service Ltd., 1985.

Mukherjea, Subimal Kumar. Bangladesh and International Law. Cal- cutta: West Bengal Political Science Association, 1971.

Naik, J. A. India, Russia, China, and Bangladesh. New Delhi:
    S. Chand, 1972.

Oliver, Thomas W. The United Nations in Bangladesh. Princeton,
    NJ: Princeton University Press, 1978.

Reza, Sadrel, and Hafiz Siddiqi. Bangladesh in South Asian and
    ASEAN: A Study in Economic Cooperation. Dhaka: Bangla-
    desh Unnayan Parishad, 1984.

Sharma, Shri Ram. Bangladesh Crisis and Indian Foreign Policy.
    n.p.: New Delhi, n.d.

Sobhan, Rehman. The Crisis of External Dependence: The Political
    Economy of Foreign Aid to Bangladesh. London: Zed Press,
    1982.

Subrahmanyam, K. Bangladesh and India's Security. Dehra Dun:
    Palit and Dutt, 1972.

Wilcox, Wayne A. The Emergence of Bangladesh: Problems and Op-
    portunities for a Redefined American Policy in South Asia.
    Washington: American Enterprise Institute, 1973.

Workshop on the Indian Ocean as a Zone of Peace, 1985. Boston:
    Martinus Nijhoff, 1986. November 23-25, 1985.

ECONOMICS

AGRICULTURE

Ahmad, Alia. Agricultural Stagnation Under Population Pressure:
    The Case of Bangladesh. Advent, NY: Vikas India, 1984.

Ahmed, Iftikhar. Technological Change and Agrarian Structure:
    A Study of Bangladesh. International Labour Office, 1981.

Bangladesh Agricultural Development Corporation. Agriculture in
    Bangladesh. Elite Printing and Packaging Ltd., Dhaka, 1987.

The Bangladesh Census of Agriculture and Livestock, 1983-84. Dhaka: Bangladesh Bureau of Statistics, Ministry of Planning, Govt. of the People's Republic of Bangladesh, 1986.

Chowdhury, Anwarullah. Agrarian Social Relations & Rural Development in Bangladesh. Allanheld, 1983.

DeVylder, Stephan. Agriculture in Chains: A Case Study in Contradictions and Constraints. London: Zed Press, 1981.

Hossain, Mahbub, and M. A. Quiddus. Some Economic Aspects of Jute Production in Bangladesh: An Inter-District Study. Dacca: Bangladesh Institute of Development Studies, 1972.

Jannuzi, F. T., and James T. Peach. The Agrarian Structure of Bangladesh. New Delhi: Orient Longman India, 1982.

Pray, Carl, and Jock R. Anderson. Bangladesh and the CGIAR Centers: A Study of Their Collaboration in Agricultural Research. Washington, DC: World Bank, 1985.

Sorenson, L. Orlo, and Do Sup Chung. Bangladesh Food Grain Storage and Stock Management Study. Prepared for the Agency for International Development, AID/TA-C-1162. Food and Feed Grain Institute, Kansas State University, 1976.

Wennergren, Boyd, Morris D. Whitaker; and Charles Antholt. Agricultural Development in Bangladesh: Prospects for the Future. Boulder, CO: Westview Press, 1984.

DEVELOPMENT, FINANCE

Ahmad, N. A. New Economic Geography of Bangladesh. New Delhi: Vikas, 1976.

Alamgir, Mohiuddin. Bangladesh: A Case of Below Poverty Level Equilibrium Trap. Dhaka: Bangladesh Institute of Development Studies, 1978.

Bangladesh: Country Study and Norwegian Aid Review. Fantoft,

Norway: Chr. Michelsen Institute, Dept. of Social Science and Development, DERAP-Development Research and Action Programme, 1986.

Bangladesh Household Expenditure Survey, 1981-82. Bureau of Statistics, Ministry of Planning, Govt. of the People's Republic of Bangladesh, Dhaka, 1986.

Bangladesh Planning Commission. The First Five Year Plan: 1973-78. Dacca: Planning Commission, 1973.

_____. The Second Five Year Plan. Dacca: Planning Commission, 1978.

_____. Economic Development in 1973-74 and Annual Plan for 1974-75. Dacca: Planning Commission, 1974.

_____. The Annual Plan, 1972-1973. Dacca: Bangladesh Government Press, 1972.

Dacca Export Fair. 3rd National Export Exposition, 1978. Dacca: Export Promotion Bureau, 1978.

Dutt, Kalyan; Runajit Dasgupta; and Anil Chatterjee. Bangladesh Economy: An Analytical Study. New Delhi: People's Publishing House, 1973.

The Economic Development of Bangladesh Within a Socialist Framework. New York: Halstead Press, 1974.

Etienne, Gilbert. Bangladesh: Development in Perspective. New Delhi: South Asia Books, 1979.

Faaland, Just, and John Richard Parkinson. Bangladesh: The Test Case for Development. Boulder, CO: Westview Press, 1976.

Farouk, A. Economic Development in Bangladesh. Dacca: Bureau of Business Research, 1974.

Islam, Nurul. Development Planning in Bangladesh: A Study in Political Economy. New York: St. Martin's Press, 1977.

_____. Development Strategy of Bangladesh. New York: Pergamon, 1977.

Jayarajah, Carl A. Bangladesh: Current Trends and Development Issues. Washington, DC: World Bank, 1979.

Khan, A. R. The Economy of Bangladesh. London: MacMillan, 1972.

Matin, K. M. Bangladesh and the IMF: An Exploratory Study. Dhaka: Bangladesh Institute of Development Studies, 1986.

Ministry of Finance. Bangladesh Economic Survey. 1979-80.

Rahim, A. M. A. (Ed.) Bangladesh Economy Problems and Issues. Dhaka: University Press, 1977.

_____. (Ed.) Bangladesh Economy: Problems and Policies. Dhaka: Barnamala Press & Publications, 1980.

Rao, V. K. R. V. Bangla Desh Economy: Problems and Prospects. Delhi: Vikas Publications, 1972.

Rehman, Sobhan. The Crisis of External Dependence: The Political Economy of Foreign Aid to Bangladesh. London: Zed, 1982.

Robinson, E. A. G. Economic Prospects of Bangladesh. London: Overseas Development Institute, 1973.

_____, and K. Griffin. The Economic Development of Bangladesh within a Socialist Framework. New York: Halstead Press, 1974.

Seth, K. L. Economic Prospects of Bangladesh. New Delhi: Trimurti Publications, 1972.

Sharma, Prakash C. Rural and Economic Development Planning in Bangladesh 1950-1972. Monticello, IL: Council of Planning Librarians, 1975.

Sirajuddin, Muhammad. Institutional Support for Planning and Project Management. Dhaka: The Pioneer Printing Press, 197- .

Stepanek, Joseph F. Bangladesh: Equitable Growth? Elmsford, NY: Pergamon Press, 1979.

Stevens, Robert D. Rural Development in Bangladesh and Pakistan. Honolulu: University of Hawaii Press, 1976.

Thomas, Winburn Townshed. Bangladesh, Views on Development Planning. Collected by Maleka Rahman, Rahman Jahangir, Mohammad Selim. Dhaka: n.p., 1983.

United Nations. International Bank for Reconstruction and Development and International Development Association. Restructuring the Economy of Bangladesh. New York: United Nations, September 1972.

Von Bottcher, Beitragen. Bangladesh im Schatten der Macht. Aufl. Aachen: Rader-Verlag, 1986.

World Bank, South Asia Regional Office. Bangladesh: Current Trends and Development Issues. Washington, DC: 1979.

Yunus, Muhammad. Planning in Bangladesh: Format, Technique, and Priority, and other essays. Rural Studies Project, Dept. of Economics, Chittagong University, 1976.

LABOR

Bangladesh: Project Findings and Recommendations. Report prepared for the Government of Bangladesh by the International Labour Organization acting as executing agency for the United Nations Development Programme. Geneva: United Nations Development Programme, International Labour Organization, 1980.

STATISTICS

Bangladesh, Bureau of Statistics. Annual Statistical Yearbook of
Bangladesh. Dacca, 1972.

Society and Commerce Publications, Economic Research Bureau. Statistical Abstract of Bangladesh. Calcutta: Society and Commerce Publications, 1972.

COMMERCE AND INDUSTRY

Alam, Ahmad Fakhrul. Problems of Export Financing in Bangladesh.
Dacca: Bureau of Economic Research, Dacca University, 1974.

Bangladesh Trade and Industry Directory, 1985. A. F. M. Shamsuz-
zaman (ed.). Dhaka: Bangladesh Chamber of Commerce and
Industry, 1985.

Chowdhury, Naimuddin. The Industry of Bangladesh: Problems and
Prospects. Dacca: Bangladesh Institute of Development
Studies, 1974.

DeLucia, R. J., and H. D. Jacoby. Energy Planning for Developing
Countries: A Study of Bangladesh. Baltimore: Johns Hop-
kins Univ. Press, 1982.

Habibullah, M. Industrial Efficiency and Profitability in Bangladesh.
Dacca: Bureau of Economic Research, Dacca University, 1974.

APPENDIX 1

LIEUTENANT GOVERNORS AND GOVERNORS OF BENGAL DURING THE BRITISH PERIOD

Lieutenant Governors

1898-1903	J. Woodburn
1903-1908	A. H. L. Fraser
1908-1912	E. N. Baker

Governors

1912-1917	Lord Carmichael
1917-1922	The Earl of Ronaldshay (later the Marquess of Zetland)
1922-1927	The Earl of Lytton
1927-1930	F. S. Jackson
1930-1932	H. L. Stephenson
1932-1937	Sir John Anderson
1937-1939	Lord Brabourne
1939-1944	Sir John Herbert
1944-1946	Lord Casey
1946-1947	F. J. Burrows

Lieutenant Governors of Eastern Bengal and Assam

1905-1906	J. B. Fuller
1906-1911	Sir Lancelot Hare
1911-1912	C. S. Bayley

GOVERNORS AND CHIEF MINISTERS
OF EAST BENGAL/EAST PAKISTAN

(Asterisk indicates individual is included in the Dictionary.)

Governors

1947-1950	Sir Frederick Bourne
1950-1953	Malik Sir Firoz Khan Noon*
1953-1954	Chaudhury Khaliquzzaman*
1954	Iskandar Mirza*
1954	Sir Thomas Ellis (acting)
1954-1955	Justice Shahabuddin*
1955-1956	Justice Amiruddin Ahmad
1956-1958	Moulvi A. K. Fazlul Haq*
1958	Hamid Ali (acting)
1958	Sultanuddin Ahmad (acting)*
1958-1960	Zakir Husain
1960-1962	Muhammad Azam Khan*
1962	Ghulam Faruque
1962-1969	Abdul Monem Khan*
1969	Mirza Nurul Huda*
1969-1971	Syed Muhammad Ahsan
1971	Abdul Mottalib Malik*

Chief Ministers

1947-1948	Khwaja Sir Nazimuddin*
1948-1954	Nurul Amin*
1954	Maulvi A. K. Fazlul Haq*
1954-1955	Under central government rule
1955-1956	Abu Husain Sarkar
1956-1958	Ataur Rahman Khan*
1958	Abu Hussain Sarkar*
1958	Ataur Rahman Khan*
1958-1971	Parliamentary system abolished

APPENDIX 3

PRINCIPAL OFFICERS OF THE GOVERNMENT OF BANGLADESH
1971-1986

MUJIB PERIOD-1971-1975

President

Dec. 1971-Jan. 1972	Sheikh Mujibur Rahman*
	(Syed Nazrul Islam*, Acting)
Jan. 1972-Dec. 1973	Abu Sayeed Chowdhury*
Jan. 1974-Jan. 1975	Mohammadullah*
Jan. 1975-Aug. 1975	Sheikh Mujibur Rahman*

Vice-President

Jan. 1975-Aug. 1975	Syed Nazrul Islam*

Prime Minister

Dec. 1971-Jan. 1972	Tajuddin Ahmad*
Jan. 1972-Jan. 1975	Sheikh Mujibur Rahman*
Jan. 1975-Aug. 1975	Mansur Ali*

Minister of Agriculture

Jan. 1972-Feb. 1972	Phani Bhushan Majumdar*
Feb. 1972-Mar. 1973	Sheikh Abdul Aziz
Apr. 1973-Aug. 1975	Muhammad Abdus Samad Azad

Minister of Commerce

Jan. 1972-Feb. 1972	Mansur Ali*
Feb. 1972-Mar. 1972	Syed Nazrul Islam*
Mar. 1972-Aug. 1975	Khondakar Mustaque Ahmed*

Minister of Communications

Jan. 1972-Feb. 1972	Sheikh Abdul Aziz
Feb. 1972-Aug. 1975	Mansur Ali*

Minister of Defense

Dec. 1971-Jan. 1972	Muhammad Ataul Ghani Osmany*
Jan. 1972-Feb. 1972	Tajuddin Ahmad*
Feb. 1972-Aug. 1975	Sheikh Mujibur Rahman*

Minister of Finance

Dec. 1971-Feb. 1972	Mansur Ali*
Feb. 1972-Nov. 1974	Tajuddin Ahmad*
Dec. 1974-Jan. 1975	vacant
Jan. 1975-Aug. 1975	Azizur Rahman Mallick

Minister of Food and Civil Supplies

Jan. 1972-June 1974	Phani Bhushan Majumdar*
July 1974-Aug. 1975	Abdul Monim

Minister of Foreign Affairs

Dec. 1971-Jan. 1972	Khondakar Mustaque Ahmed*
Jan. 1972-Mar. 1973	Muhammad Abdus Samad Azad
Apr. 1973-Aug. 1975	Kamal Hossain*

Minister of Foreign Trade

(Included with Minister of Commerce except below)

Apr. 1973-Feb. 1974	A. H. M. Kamaruzzaman*

Minister of Forests, Fisheries and Livestock

Apr. 1972-Mar. 1973	Muhammad Sohrab Hossain
Apr. 1973-Jan. 1974	Abdur Rab Serniabat*
Feb. 1974-Feb. 1974	Mollah Jalaluddin Ahmad*
Mar. 1974-June 1974	Sheikh Mujibur Rahman*
July 1974-Nov. 1974	Tajuddin Ahmad*
Dec. 1974	vacant
Jan. 1975-Aug. 1975	Abdur Rab Serniabat*

Minister of Health and Family Planning

Jan. 1972-Mar. 1972	Zahur Ahmad Chowdhury
Apr. 1972-Mar. 1973	Abdul Malik Ukil
Apr. 1973-Aug. 1975	Abdul Mannan

Minister of Home Affairs

Dec. 1971-Feb. 1972	A. H. M. Kamaruzzaman*
Feb. 1972-Mar. 1972	Sheikh Mujibur Rahman*
Apr. 1972-Mar. 1973	Abdul Mannan
Apr. 1973-June 1974	Abdul Malik Ukil
July 1974-Aug. 1975	Mansur Ali*

Minister of Industries

Dec. 1972-Feb. 1972	Mansur Ali*
Feb. 1972-Mar. 1972	Syed Nazrul Islam*
Apr. 1972-Mar. 1973	Mustifizur Rahman Siddiqui
Apr. 1973-Feb. 1974	A. H. M. Kamaruzzaman*
Mar. 1974-Aug. 1975	Syed Nazrul Islam*

Minister of Information and Broadcasting

Jan. 1972-Feb. 1972	Tajuddin Ahmad*
Feb. 1972-Mar. 1972	Sheikh Mujibur Rahman*
Apr. 1972-Mar. 1973	Mizanur Rahman Choudhury*
Apr. 1973-Sep. 1973	Sheikh Abdul Aziz
Oct. 1973-Jan. 1975	Sheikh Mujibur Rahman*
Jan. 1975-Aug. 1975	Korban Ali

Minister of Jute

Apr. 1973-June 1974	Tajuddin Ahmad*
July 1974-Jan. 1975	Sheikh Mujibur Rahman*
Jan. 1975-Aug. 1975	Asaduzzaman Khan

Minister of Labor and Social Welfare

Jan. 1972-June 1974	Zahur Ahmad Chowdhury
July 1974-Jan. 1975	Abdul Mannan
Jan. 1975-Aug. 1975	Muhammad Yusuf Ali

Minister of Land Revenue

(After Mar. 1974, titled Minister of Land Administration and Land Reform)

Jan. 1972-Mar. 1972	Khondakar Mustaque Ahmed*
Apr. 1972-Feb. 1974	Abdur Rab Serniabat*
Mar. 1974-June 1974	Mollah Jalaluddin Ahmad*
July 1974-Jan. 1975	Phani Bhushan Majumdar*
Jan. 1975-Aug. 1975	Mohammadullah*

Minister of Law, Parliamentary Affairs and Justice

Jan. 1972-Feb. 1972	Khondakar Mustaque Ahmed*
Feb. 1972-Mar. 1973	Kamal Hossain*
Apr. 1973-Aug. 1975	Manoranjan Dhar

Minister of Local Government, Rural Development and Cooperatives

Jan. 1972-Feb. 1972	Phani Bhushan Majumdar*
Feb. 1972-Mar. 1972	Sheikh Abdul Aziz
Apr. 1972-Mar. 1973	Shamsul Haq
Apr. 1973-June 1974	Matiur Rahman
July 1974-Jan. 1975	Muhammad Abdus Samad Azad
Jan. 1975-Aug. 1975	Phani Bhushan Majumdar*

Minister of Planning

Jan. 1972-Nov. 1974	Tajuddin Ahmad*
Dec. 1974-Jan. 1975	vacant
Jan. 1975-Aug. 1975	Syed Nazrul Islam*

Minister of Posts, Telephones and Telegraph

Apr. 1972-Mar. 1973	Mollah Jalaluddin Ahmad*
Apr. 1973-Sep. 1973	Mohammad Ataul Ghani Osmany*
Oct. 1973-June 1974	Sheikh Abdul Aziz
July 1974-Aug. 1975	Mansur Ali*

Minister of Power, Natural Resources, Scientific and Technological Research and Atomic Energy

(Title varied; Power dropped in Mar. 1974)

Apr. 1972-June 1974	Mafiz Ahmad Choudhury
July 1974-Jan. 1975	Kamal Hossain*

Jan. 1975-Aug. 1975   Remaining divisions included with
                             Education

Minister of Power, Flood Control and Irrigation

(Title varied)

Feb. 1972-Feb. 1974   Khondakar Mushtaque Ahmad*
Mar. 1974-Aug. 1975   Abdur Rab Serniabat*

Minister of Public Works and Housing

Jan. 1972-Feb. 1972   Muhammad Yusuf Ali
Feb. 1972-Mar. 1972   Kamal Hossain*
Apr. 1972-Mar. 1973   Matiur Rahman
Apr. 1973-Aug. 1975   Mohammad Sohrab Hossain

Minister of Relief and Rehabilitation

Dec. 1971-Mar. 1973   A. H. M. Kamaruzzaman*
Apr. 1973-May 1973   Mizanur Rahman Chowdhury*
June 1973-June 1974   Sheikh Mujibur Rahman*
July 1974-Aug. 1975   Abdul Monim

Minister of Shipping, Inland Waterways and Water Transport

Apr. 1972-June 1974   Mohammad Ataul Ghani Osmany*
July 1974-Jan. 1975   Sheikh Mujibur Rahman*
Jan. 1975-Aug. 1975   Mansur Ali*
Aug. 1975   Abu Sayeed Choudhury*

MUSHTAQUE INTERREGNUM
(August-November 1975)

President: Khondakar Mustaque Ahmed*

Vice President: Mohammadullah*

Ministers

Agriculture: Abdul Monim
Defense: Khondakar Mushtaque Ahmad*
Education, Scientific and Technological Research and Atomic Energy:
  Muzaffar Ahmad Choudhury

Finance: Azizur Rahman Mallick
Food: Abdul Monim
Foreign Affairs: Abu Sayeed Chowdhury*
Health and Family Planning: Abdul Mannan
Home Affairs: Khondakar Mustaque Ahmed*
Law, Parliamentary Affairs and Justice: Manoranjan Dhar
Local Government, Rural Development and Cooperatives: Phani
    Bhushan Majumdar*
Planning: Muhammad Yusuf Ali
Ports, Shipping and Inland Water Transport: Asaduzzaman Khan
Public Works and Urban Development: Mohammad Sohrab Hossain
Relief and Rehabilitation: Khitish Chandra Mondal

ZIA PERIOD
(1975-1982, including the period of Abdus Sattar)

President

Nov. 1975-Apr. 1977	Abu Sadat Muhammad Sayem*
Apr. 1977-May 1981	Ziaur Rahman*
May 1981-Mar. 1982	Abdus Sattar*

Vice-President

June 1977-May 1981	Abdus Sattar*
Nov. 1981-Mar. 1982	Mirza Nurul Huda*
Mar. 1982	Mohammadullah*

Chief Martial Law Administrator

| Nov. 1975-Nov. 1976 | Abu Sadat Muhammad Sayem* |
| Nov. 1976-Mar. 1979 | Ziaur Rahman* |

Deputy Chief Martial Law Administrators

Nov. 1975-Nov. 1976	Ziaur Rahman*
Nov. 1975-Nov. 1977	Mosharraf Hossain Khan
Nov. 1975-Apr. 1976	Muhammad Ghulam Tawab
May 1976-Sep. 1976	Mohammad Khademul Bashar
Sep. 1976-Nov. 1977	Abdul Ghaffar Mahmud

Prime Minister

| Mar. 1979-Mar. 1982 | Shah Azizur Rahman* |

Deputy Prime Ministers

Apr. 1979-Aug. 1979	A. Q. M. Badruddoza Choudhury
Apr. 1979-Dec. 1979	Moudud Ahmad*
Sep. 1979-Jan. 1982	Jamaluddin Ahmad
Sep. 1979-Dec. 1981	S. A. Bari A.T.

Minister of Agriculture

(Includes Forests except where separate entry is given.)

Nov. 1975-Nov. 1975	Muhammad Ghulam Tawab*
Dec. 1975-Jan. 1976	Abu Sadat Muhammad Sayem*
Feb. 1976-June 1976	Mirza Nurul Huda*
July 1976-Mar. 1979	Azizul Haq
Apr. 1979-Dec. 1981	Nurul Islam
Jan. 1982	Fasihuddin Mahtab
Feb. 1982	Abdul Halim Chowdhury
Mar. 1982	Riazuddin Ahmad

Minister of Civil Aviation and Tourism

Nov. 1975-Jan. 1976	Muhammad Ghulam Tawab*
Feb. 1976-Dec. 1976	Included with Communications
Jan. 1977-June 1978	Abdul Ghaffar Mahmud
July 1978-Mar. 1979	Kazi Anwarul Haque
Apr. 1979-Aug. 1979	M. A. Matin
Sep. 1979-Apr. 1980	Kazi Anwarul Haque
May 1980-Dec. 1981	K. M. Obaidur Rahman
Jan. 1982-Mar. 1982	A. K. M. Moidul Islam

Minister of Commerce

(Included Foreign Trade until Feb. 1978)

Nov. 1975-Nov. 1975	Ziaur Rahman*
Dec. 1975-Dec. 1976	Mirza Nurul Huda*
Jan. 1977-Apr. 1980	Mohammad Saifur Rahman
May 1980-Dec. 1981	vacant
Jan. 1982	A. S. M. Mustafizur Rahman
Feb. 1982-Mar. 1982	Mirza Nurul Huda*

Minister of Communications

Nov. 1975-Nov. 1975	Musharraf Hossain Khan
Dec. 1975-Jan. 1976	Kazi Anwarul Haque
Feb. 1976-Nov. 1977	Mosharraf Hossain Khan

(After Nov. 1977 divided into several ministries.)

Minister of Defense

Nov. 1975-Apr. 1977	Abu Sadat Muhammad Sayem*
May 1977-May 1981	Ziaur Rahman*
May 1981-Mar. 1982	Abdus Sattar*

Minister of Education

Nov. 1975-Nov. 1975	Ziaur Rahman*
Dec. 1975-June 1977	Abul Fazal
July 1977-June 1978	Syed Ali Ahsan
July 1978-Oct. 1978	Kazi Zafar Ahmad
Nov. 1978-Mar. 1979	Abdul Baten
Apr. 1979-Jan. 1982	Shah Azizur Rahman*
Feb. 1982-Mar. 1982	Tofazzul Husain Khan

Minister in charge of the Establishment Division

Nov. 1977-June 1978	Ziaur Rahman*
July 1978-Jan. 1982	Mohammad Majidul Huq
Feb. 1982-Mar. 1982	Abdus Sattar*

Minister of Finance

Nov. 1975-Nov. 1978	Ziaur Rahman*
Dec. 1978-Apr. 1980	Mirza Nurul Huda*
May 1980-Jan. 1982	Mohammad Saifur Rahman
Feb. 1982-Mar. 1982	Fasihuddin Mahtab

Minister of Fisheries and Livestock

Nov. 1975-Jan. 1976	Mosharraf Hossain Khan (included Forests)
Feb. 1976-Nov. 1977	Included in Agriculture
Dec. 1977-June 1978	M. R. Khan
July 1978-Apr. 1980	K. M. Obaidur Rahman
May 1980-Jan. 1982	S. A. Bari A.T.
Feb. 1982-Mar. 1982	at minister of state level

Minister of Food

Nov. 1975-Apr. 1976	Muhammad Ghulam Tawab*
May 1976-Aug. 1976	Mohammad Khademul Bashar

Aug. 1976-June 1977	Abdul Ghaffar Mahmud
July 1977-Jan. 1982	Abdul Momen Khan
Feb. 1982-Mar. 1982	Abdul Halim Chowdhury

Minister of Foreign Affairs

Nov. 1975-Mar. 1977	Abu Sadat Muhammad Sayem*
Apr. 1977-Mar. 1982	Muhammad Shamsul Huq*

Minister of Health and Population Control

Nov. 1975-Nov. 1975	Muhammad Ghulam Tawab*
Dec. 1975-Nov. 1977	Mohammad Ibrahim (from July 1977 to Aug. 1977, Ibrahim held only Population Control; Mohammad Masudul Haque held Health, Labor and Social Welfare.)
Dec. 1977-Aug. 1979	A. Q. M. Badruddoza Choudhury
Sep. 1979-Mar. 1981	M. A. Matin
May. 1981-June 1981	vacant
July 1981-Dec. 1981	M. A. Matin
Jan. 1982	Abdur Rahman Biswas
Feb. 1982-Mar. 1982	Khondker Abdul Hamid

Minister of Home Affairs

Nov. 1975-June 1978	Ziaur Rahman*
July 1978-Dec. 1981	A. S. M. Mustafizur Rahman
Jan. 1982-Mar. 1982	M. A. Matin

Minister of Industries

Nov. 1975-Nov. 1975	Ziaur Rahman*
Dec. 1975-Jan. 1976	Mirza Nurul Huda*
Feb. 1976-June 1977	A. K. M. Hafizuddin
July 1977-Jan. 1982	Jamaluddin Ahmad
Feb. 1982	Mirza Nurul Huda*
Mar. 1982	Muhammad Yusuf Ali

Minister of Information and Broadcasting

Nov. 1975-Sep. 1976	Ziaur Rahman*
Oct. 1976-Oct. 1977	Akbar Kabir
Nov. 1977-June 1978	Shamsul Huda Chowdhury
July 1978-Apr. 1980	Habibullah Khan
May 1980-Jan. 1982	Shamsul Huda Chowdhury

Feb. 1982	Tofazzul Husain Khan
Mar. 1982	Shamsul Huda Chowdhury

Minister of Jute

Nov. 1975-Nov. 1975	Ziaur Rahman*
Dec. 1975-July 1977	Kazi Anwarul Haque
Aug. 1977-Mar. 1979	S. M. Shafiul Azam
Apr. 1979-Apr. 1980	Abdur Rahman Biswas
May 1980-Dec. 1981	Habibullah Khan
Jan. 1982-Mar. 1982	Muhammad Yusuf Ali

Minister of Labor

(At times included Social Welfare)

Nov. 1975-Nov. 1975	Mosharraf Hossain Khan
Dec. 1975-Jan. 1976	Abul Fazal
Feb. 1976-June 1976	Mohammad Ibrahim
July 1976-Jan. 1977	Mohammad Masudul Haque
Feb. 1977-Aug. 1977	Included with Health
Sep. 1977-June 1978	Included with Manpower Development
July 1978-Apr. 1979	Shah Azizur Rahman*
May 1979-Aug. 1979	vacant
Sep. 1979-Jan. 1982	Riazuddin Ahmad
Feb. 1982-Mar. 1982	Khondker Abdul Hamid

Minister of Land Administration and Land Reforms

Nov. 1975-Nov. 1975	Mosharraf Hossain Khan
Dec. 1975-Jan. 1976	Mrs. Benita Roy
Feb. 1976-Nov. 1977	Kazi Anwarul Haque
Dec. 1977-June 1978	Enayetullah Khan
July 1978-Mar. 1979	Mirza Ghulam Hafiz
Apr. 1979-Jan. 1982	Mohammad Abdul Haque
Feb. 1982	Abdus Sattar*
Mar. 1982	Tofazzul Husain Khan

Minister of Law, Parliamentary Affairs and Justice

Nov. 1975-Jan. 1977	Abu Sadat Mohammad Sayem*
Feb. 1977-Dec. 1981	Abdus Sattar*
Jan. 1982	Tofazzul Husain Khan
Feb. 1982-Mar. 1982	Shah Azizur Rahman*

Minister of Local Government, Rural Development and Cooperatives

Nov. 1975-Nov. 1975	Muhammad Ghulam Tawab*
Dec. 1975-Jan. 1976	Mohammad Abdur Rashid
Feb. 1976-June 1978	Kazi Anwarul Haque
July 1978-Jan. 1982	Abdul Halim Chaudhury
Feb. 1982-Mar. 1982	Shah Azizur Rahman*

Minister of Manpower Development and Social Welfare

Nov. 1975-Aug. 1977	Under other ministries
Sept. 1977-Nov. 1977	Mohamad Majidul Haque
Dec. 1977-June 1978	Zakaria Chowhury
July 1978-Jan. 1982	S. A. Bari A.T.
Feb. 1982-Mar. 1982	to Ministry of Labor

Minister of Petroleum and Natural Resources

Nov. 1975-Apr. 1976	Mohammad Ghulam Tawab*
May 1976-Aug. 1976	Mohammad Khademul Bashar
Aug. 1976-June 1977	Abdul Ghaffar Mahmud
July 1977-June 1978	Ashfaque Hussain Khan
July 1978-Oct. 1978	Enayetullah Khan
Nov. 1978-June 1981	Akbar Hussain
July 1981-Jan. 1982	Kazi Anwarul Haque
Feb. 1982-Mar. 1982	vacant

Minister of Planning

Nov. 1975-Nov. 1975	Abu Sadat Muhammad Sayem*
Dec. 1975-Apr. 1979	Mirza Nurul Huda*
May 1979-Dec. 1981	Fasihuddin Mahtab
Jan. 1982-Mar. 1982	Abdus Sattar*

Minister of Ports, Shipping and Inland Water Transport

Nov. 1975-Jan. 1976	Mosharraf Hossain Khan
Feb. 1976-Nov. 1977	Included in Communications
Dec. 1977-Dec. 1981	Nurul Huq
Jan. 1982	vacant
Feb. 1982	Shamsul Huda Chowdhury
Mar. 1982	Sultan Ahmad Chowdhury

Minister of Posts, Telegraph and Telephones

Nov. 1975-Jan. 1976	Muhammad Ghulam Tawab*

Feb. 1976-Nov. 1977	Included in Communications
Dec. 1977-Mar. 1979	Moudud Ahmad*
Apr. 1979-Feb. 1982	A. K. M. Moidul Islam
Mar. 1982	Sultan Ahmad Chowdhury

Minister of Power, Flood Control and Water Resources

Nov. 1975-Nov. 1977	Mosharraf Hossain Khan
Dec. 1977-Mar. 1979	B. M. Abbas A.T.
Apr. 1979-Dec. 1979	Moudud Ahmad*
Jan. 1980-Dec. 1981	Kazi Anwarul Haque
Jan. 1982	I. K. Siddiqui
Feb. 1982	vacant
Mar. 1982	Abdus Sattar*

Minister of Public Works and Urban Development

Nov. 1975-Nov. 1975	Muhammad Ghulam Tawab*
Dec. 1975-June 1978	Mohammad Abdur Rashid
July 1978-Apr. 1980	Abdur Rahman
May 1980-May 1981	vacant
June 1981-Jan. 1982	Abul Hasnat
Feb. 1982-Mar. 1982	vacant

Minister of Railways, Roads, Highways and Road Transport

Dec. 1975-Dec. 1975	Kazi Anwarul Haque
Jan. 1976-Nov. 1977	Included with Communications
Dec. 1977-June 1978	Mohammad Majidul Huq
July 1978-Feb. 1979	Mashiur Rahman*
Mar. 1979-Apr. 1979	vacant
May 1979-Jan. 1982	Abdul Alim
Feb. 1982-Mar. 1982	Shamsul Huda Chowdhury

Minister of Relief and Rehabilitation

Nov. 1975-Nov. 1975	Mohammad Ghulam Tawab*
Dec. 1975-Jan. 1976	Muhammad Abdur Rashid
Feb. 1976-June 1978	Mrs. Benita Roy
July 1978-Mar. 1979	Rasa Raj Mondal
Apr. 1979-Jan. 1982	Imran Ali Sarkar
Feb. 1982-Mar. 1982	vacant

Minister of Science and Technology

Nov. 1975-Nov. 1975	Ziaur Rahman*

Dec. 1975-Jan. 1976	Abul Fazal
Feb. 1976-May 1981	Ziaur Rahman*
May 1981-Mar. 1982	Abdus Sattar*

Minister of Sports, Cultural Affairs and Religion

(title varies; Religion added in May, 1979)

July 1978-Jan. 1982	Shamsul Huda Choudhury
Feb. 1982	Tofazzul Husain Khan
Mar. 1982	Shamsul Huda Chowdhury

Minister of Textiles

Nov. 1975-June 1977	Included with Industry
July 1977-June 1978	Muzaffar Ahmad
July 1978-Mar. 1979	Abdul Alim
Apr. 1979-Mar. 1981	Mansur Ali
Apr. 1981-Mar. 1982	Muhammad Yusuf Ali

Minister of Women's Affairs

July 1978-Apr. 1980	Mrs. Amina Rahman
May 1980-Mar. 1982	vacant

Minister of Youth Development

July 1978-Mar. 1979	Kazi Anwarul Haque
Apr. 1979-Apr. 1980	Khondakar Abdul Hamid
May 1980-Mar. 1981	Abdus Sattar*
Apr. 1981-Dec. 1981	M. A. Matin
Jan. 1982	Abul Qasim
Feb. 1982-Mar. 1982	vacant

ERSHAD PERIOD
(Through August 1986)

President

Mar. 1982-May 1984	A. F. M. Ahsanuddin Chowdhury*
June 1984-	Hussain Muhammad Ershad*

Chief Martial Law Administrator

Mar. 1982-   Hussain Muhammad Ershad*

Prime Minister

Mar. 1984-Jan. 1985   Ataur Rahman Khan*
July 1986-   Mizanur Rahman Choudhury*

Minister of Agriculture

July 1982-June 1984   A. Z. M. Obaidullah Khan
July 1984   Mahboob Ali Khan
Feb. 1985-   Munhmmad Abdul Munim

Minister of Civil Aviation and Tourism

Aug. 1982-Jan. 1985   Hussain Muhammad Ershad*
Feb. 1985-Oct. 1985   A. R. Yusuf
July 1986-   Shafiqul Ghani Swapan

Minister of Commerce

May 1982-Apr. 1984   Shafiul Azam
May 1984-Jan. 1985   M. A. Matin
Feb. 1985-May 1985   Sultan Mahmud
June 1985-Apr. 1986   Kazi Zafar Ahmad
May 1986-June 1986   Sultan Mahmud
July 1986-   Kazi Zafar Ahmad

Minister of Communications

Mar. 1982-June 1984   Mahboob Ali Khan
July 1984-Jan. 1985   A. Z. M. Obaidullah Khan
Feb. 1985-Oct. 1985   Sultan Ahmad
Nov. 1985-Apr. 1986   Moudud Ahmad*
May 1986-June 1986   Sultan Ahmad
July 1986-   M. A. Matin

Minister of Defense

Apr. 1982-   Hussain Muhammad Ershad*

Minister of Education

June 1982-June 1984	Abdul Majeed Khan
July 1984-Jan. 1985	Shamsul Huda Chowdhury
Feb. 1985-Oct. 1985	Hussain Muhammad Ershad*
Nov. 1985-Feb. 1986	Shamsul Huda Chowdhury
Mar. 1986-Apr. 1986	M. A. Matin
May 1986-June 1986	Nurul Islam
July 1986-	Mominuddin Ahmad

Minister of Energy and Mineral Resources

Mar. 1982-Apr. 1982	Abdul Gaffar Mahmud
May 1982-July 1984	Sultan Mahmud
Feb. 1985-May 1985	Hussain Muhammad Ershad*
June 1985-Apr. 1986	Anwar Hossain
May 1986-June 1986	Muhammad Abdul Munim
July 1986-	Anwar Hossain

Minister of Establishment and Reorganization

Oct. 1983-Jan. 1985	Mohabat Jan Chowdhury
Feb. 1985-	Hussain Muhammad Ershad*

Minister of Finance

Mar. 1982-Jan. 1984	Abul Maal Abdul Muhith
Feb. 1984-	Hussain Muhammad Ershad*

Minister of Fisheries and Animal Husbandry

Nov. 1985-Apr. 1986	Sirajul Hussain Khan
May 1986-June 1986	Abdul Mannan Siddiqui
July 1986-	Sirajul Hussain Khan

Minister of Food

Apr. 1982-Jan. 1985	Abdul Gaffar Mahmud
Feb. 1985-Apr. 1986	Mohabbat Jan Chowdhury
May 1986-June 1986	Abdul Mannan Siddiqui
July 1986-	Mohabbat Jan Chowdhury

Minister of Foreign Affairs

May 1982-June 1984	A. R. S. Doha

July 1984-May 1985   Hussain Muhammad Ershad*
June 1985-Apr. 1986   Humayun Rashid Choudhury
May 1986-June 1986   Hussain Muhammad Ershad*
July 1986-   Humayun Rashid Choudhury

Minister of Health and Family Planning

Mar. 1982-Apr. 1986   Shamsul Huq
July 1986-   Salahuddin Qadir Chowdhury

Minister of Home Affairs

Sep. 1982-Sep. 1983   Mohabbat Jan Chowdhury
Oct. 1983-Feb. 1986   Abdul Mannan Siddiqui
Mar. 1986-   Mahmudul Hasan

Minister of Industries

Mar. 1982-June 1984   Shafiul Azam
July 1984-June 1986   Sultan Mahmud
July 1986-   Moudud Ahmad*

Minister of Information and Broadcasting

Mar. 1982-May 1982   A. R. S. Doha
July 1982-Mar. 1984   Syed Najmuddin Hashim
Apr. 1984-Jan. 1985   Shamsul Huq
Feb. 1985-June 1985   A. R. Yusuf
July 1985-Oct. 1985   Serajul Hussain Khan
Nov. 1985-June 1986   Moazzem Hussain
July 1986-   Anwar Zahid

Minister of Irrigation, Water Development and Flood Control

Mar. 1982-Apr. 1982   Abdul Gaffar Mahmud
May 1982-June 1983   Sultan Mahmud
July 1983-June 1984   A. Z. M. Obaidullah Khan
July 1984   A. R. S. Doha
Aug. 1984-Jan. 1985   Muhammad Aminul Islam Khan
Feb. 1985-June 1985   Sultan Ahmad
July 1985-Oct. 1985   Muhammad Aminul Islam Khan
Nov. 1985-Apr. 1986   Anisul Islam Mahmud
May 1986-June 1986   Sultan Ahmad
July 1986-   Anisul Islam Mahmud

Minister of Jute and Textiles

July 1984	Muhammad Aminul Islam Khan
Aug. 1984-Jan. 1985	Muhammad Korban Ali
Feb. 1985-June 1985	Sultan Ahmad
July 1985-Apr. 1986	Muhammad Abdus Sattar
May 1986-June 1986	Sultan Mahmud
July 1986-	Hashimuddin Ahmad

Minister of Labor and Manpower

Mar. 1982-June 1984	Muhammad Aminul Islam Khan
July 1984-Jan. 1985	Shah Moazzem Hossain
Feb. 1985-Oct. 1985	Anisul Islam Mahmud
Nov. 1985-June 1986	Muhammad Korban Ali
July 1986-	Muhammad Abdus Sattar

Minister of Land Administration and Land Reforms

Mar. 1982-Mar. 1984	Khondakar Abu Bakr
Apr. 1984-Jan. 1985	M. A. Haq
Feb. 1985-June 1985	T. I. M. Fazle Rabbi Chowdhury
July 1985-Oct. 1985	Muhammad Korban Ali
Nov. 1985-Apr. 1986	A. K. M. Mayeedul Islam
May 1986-June 1986	Zakir Khan Chowdhury
July 1986-	Mirza Rahul Amin

Minister of Law and Justice

Mar. 1982-Mar. 1984	Khondakar Abu Bakr
July 1984-Jan. 1985	Ataur Rahman Khan*
Feb. 1985-Feb. 1986	A. K. M. Nurul Islam
Mar. 1986-Apr. 1986	A. K. M. Aminul Islam
May 1986-	A. K. M. Nurul Islam

Minister of Local Government, Rural Development and Cooperatives

Mar. 1982-Jan. 1985	Mahbubur Rahman
Feb. 1985-Feb. 1986	Mahmudul Hasan
Mar. 1986-Apr. 1986	Amanul Islam
May 1986-June 1986	Mahmudul Hasan
July 1986-	Shah Moazzem Hossain

Minister of Planning

Mar. 1982-Jan. 1984	Abul Maal Abdul Muhith

Apr. 1984-June 1984 Shamsul Huda Chowdhury
July 1984-Oct. 1985 Abdul Majeed Khan
Nov. 1985-Apr. 1986 Sultan Ahmad Chowdhury
July 1986- Muhammad Shamsul Haq

Minister of Ports, Shipping and Water Transport

Aug. 1984-Jan. 1985 Reazuddin Ahmad
Feb. 1985-Oct. 1985 Sultan Ahmad
Nov. 1985-Apr. 1986 Moudud Ahmad*
May 1986-June 1986 Sultan Ahmad
July 1986- A. K. M. Mayeedul Islam

Minister of Posts and Telegraph

Nov. 1985-Feb. 1986 Mizanur Rahman Chowdhury*
May 1986-June 1986 Sultan Ahmad
July 1986- Mizanur Rahman Chowdhury*

Minister of Relief and Rehabilitation

Apr. 1982-July 1984 Abdul Gaffar Mahmud
Aug. 1984-Jan. 1985 Muhammad Yusuf Ali
Feb. 1985-June 1985 Husain Muhammad Ershad*
July 1985-Oct. 1985 T. I. M. Fazle Rabbi Chowdhury
Nov. 1985-Feb. 1986 Salahuddin Qadir Chowdhury
Mar. 1986-June 1986 Abdul Mannan Siddiqui
July 1986- Muhammad Shamsul Haq

Minister of Religious Affairs and Endowments

June 1982-May 1983 Abdul Majeed Khan
June 1983-June 1984 Mahbubur Rahman
July 1984-Jan. 1985 Khondakar Abu Bakr
Feb. 1985-June 1985 Husain Muhammad Ershad*
July 1985-Oct. 1985 A. K. M. Nurul Islam
Nov. 1985-Feb. 1986 Muhammad Aminul Islam Khan
Mar. 1986-Apr. 1986 Shamsul Huda Chowdhury
May 1986-June 1986 A. K. M. Nurul Islam
July 1986- Maulana M. A. Mannan

Minister of Social Welfare and Women's Affairs

Apr. 1982-Jan. 1985 Shafia Khatun
Feb. 1985-June 1985 Husain Muhammad Ershad*
July 1985- Rabia Bhuiyan

Minister of Works

Mar. 1982-Sep. 1983	Abdul Mannan Siddiqui
Oct. 1983-Jan. 1985	Muhammad Abdul Munim
Feb. 1985-June 1985	Mahmudul Hasan
July 1985-Feb. 1986	M. A. Matin
Mar. 1986-Apr. 1986	Salahuddin Qadir Chowdhury
May 1986-June 1986	Muhammad Abdul Munim
July 1986-	A. K. M. Aminul Islam

Minister of Youth and Sports

July 1985-June 1986	Zakir Khan Chowdhury
July 1986-	Sunil Upta

Ministers without portfolio

Apr. 1984	Syed Najmuddin Hashim
Nov. 1984-Jan. 1985	Mizanur Rahman Chowdhury*

Source: The serial publication Chiefs of State and Cabinet Members of Foreign Governments produced by the Directorate of Intelligence, Central Intelligence Agency. The serial is either monthly or bimonthly. Dates entered in the list are those of the issue in which the name first appeared. It may not be the actual date on which the office was assumed by the individual.

In early phase of the Ershad period many portfolios were not held separately but were grouped with other portfolios. There were also frequent vacancies during which Ershad or another of the military officers held charge of the ministries.